Cherokee Removal:
Forts Along the Georgia Trail of Tears

Draft Report

By

Sarah H. Hill

Under a joint partnership between
The National Park Service and the
Georgia Department of Natural Resources/Historic Preservation Division

Funded by
The National Park Service Challenge Cost Share Program

March 2005

Acknowledgements

This project was managed by Georgia Department of Natural Resources/Historic Preservation Division staff Christine Neal and Dave Crass; maps were produced by Joey Charles. The Georgia Chapter of the Trail of Tears Association, and in particular Doug Mabry, were instrumental in helping to locate documentary material and sites. Patsy Edgar, Past President of the Georgia Chapter of the TOTA, was a tireless advocate of this project. We especially wish to thank National Trail of Tears Association President Jack Baker, whose good offices and leadership mean so much to the preservation of Trail of Tears sites throughout the southeast.

Table of Contents

Acknowledgments..ii
List of Figures v

An Introduction to the Trail of Tears Project...1

    Goals and Method 1

The Cherokee Nation in Georgia...3

    An Overview 3
        Physiography..3
        Environment and Ecology...5
        Changing Landscapes and Economies...8
        Roads and Trails 10
            The Georgia or Federal Road...10
            Postal Roads...13
            The Unicoi Turnpike...14
            The Alabama Roads...14
            The Brainerd Roads 17
            Dahlonega to the Federal Road...17
            Tennessee to Hightower River Turnpike 18
            Auraria to Northern Boundary Line of Georgia 18
            The Laudsville to Blairsville Road 19
            North Carolina to Clarksville..19
            To the North Carolina Line...19
            New Road Cut by Removal Troops 20
        Cherokee Removal in Georgia..20
        Forts and Stations...23
            Fort Wool 23
            Fort Buffington (Canton, Cherokee County)...................................28
            Sixes (Cherokee County) 31
            Fort Floyd (Dahlonega, Lumpkin County).......................................34
            Fort Hetzel (Ellijay, Gilmer County)...37
            Fort Gilmer (Rock Springs, Murray County) 39
            Fort Newnan (Blaine, Pickens County) 43
            Encampment at Chastain's (Blue Ridge, Union County) 46
            Fort Hoskins (Springplace, Murray County) 47
            Fort Campbell (Blaine, Forsythe County) 51
            Fort Cumming (Lafayette, Walker County)......................................54
            Fort Means (Kingston, Floyd County)..58
            Cedar Town (Polk County)...60
            Camp Scott (Rome, Floyd County) 63
            Perkins, Dade County 65

Archaeological Reconnaissance: Certification and Research......................74

    Goals and Methods 74

        Fort Buffington 74

        Fort Campbell 75

        Cedar Town Station 75

        Chastain's Station 75

        Fort Cumming...75

        Fort Floyd..76

        Fort Gilmer...76

        Fort Hetzel 76

        Fort Hoskins..76

        Fort Means 77

        Fort Newnan..77

        Perkins Encampment 77

        Rome Encampment 77

        Sixes Encampment...78

        Fort Wool 78

    Future Research 78

Appendix: Georgia Site Forms

List of Illustrations

Illustration 1.   The Cherokee Nation 3

Illustration 2.   Physiography of Georgia 4

Illustration 3.   Georgia Counties 5

Illustration 4.   Georgia roads and trails 10

Illustration 5.   The Vann Tavern 11

Illustration 6.   Tanner's 1834 map 12

Illustration 7.   Cherokee County in 1846 15

Illustration 8.   An 1834 map of Cherokee County 15

Illustration 9.   Paulding County in 1846 16

Illustration 10.   Walker County in 1839 17

Illustration 11.   Habersham County in 1846 19

Illustration 12.   John Ridge, Elias Boudinot, Major Ridge 21

Illustration 13.   General Winfield Scott 26

Illustration 14.   Harmony Primitive Baptist Church 28

Illustration 15.   Possible location of Fort Buffington...30

Illustration 16.   Fort Hetzel marker 37

Illustration 17.   The Vann House 40

Illustration 18.   Fort Gilmer historical marker 40

Illustration 19.   Possible location of Fort Campbell...51

Illustration 20.   Fort Cumming historical marker...55

An Introduction to the Trail of Tears Project

Goals and Methods

The goal of this project was to carry out an intensive documents review of military sites associated with the Trail of Tears in Georgia. This research was followed by a reconnaissance-level archaeological field survey of those sites on the ground. The results of the documents review and field surveys were then used to develop recommendations for certification by the National Park Service (NPS) Long Distance Trails Office, as well as recommendations for further, more intensive archaeological field study. The project was completed under a Challenge Cost Share Agreement between the NPS and the Georgia Department of Natural Resources Historic Preservation Division.

The project was conducted in two phases. During Phase I, a variety of primary and secondary sources were consulted. Removal records at the Georgia Department of Archives and History, and National Archives Record Groups 393 and 92 were particularly useful. During the documents review for each site, completed by the senior author, letters were sent to property owners in the survey area requesting permission to visit their property and to review any information that they might have gathered. The documents review phase of the project was extremely successful. In fact, so many new sources of information were discovered that the NPS kindly extended the project so that we could do a thorough review. The documents review provide the basis for the Historical Narrative: The Cherokee Nation in Georgia and Archaeological Reconnaissance: Certification and Research presented in this document.

During Phase II, we conducted reconnaissance-level surveys and field visits at locations based on the documentary evidence. Unfortunately, in many cases there was insufficient documentary evidence to precisely locate the former post. Fort Perkins, known only to be located in Dade County, is one such example. In other cases, there was good information about the possible location of a former fort. Unfortunately, the site was often inundated or destroyed by recent development. Chastain's Station, submerged by Lake Allatoona, and the station at Rome, which is probably under the modern city, are two such examples. Finally, in some cases there was relatively good information about location, but we were unable to secure permission to carry out a survey in order to locate high-probability areas. Fort Campbell is an example of this type of property. While it is not surprising that we were unable to secure permission to enter many tracts given the strong private property ethic in north Georgia, it was nevertheless disappointing.

Field pedestrian surveys were oriented toward locating high-probability landforms, generally considered to be relatively high ground near water sources. Where possible, shovel testing or bucket auger testing was carried out to assess whether there was a viable A horizon (topsoil), which would indicate potential for intact subsurface archaeological deposits. Where permission to enter a property was not secured or the precise relocation of the fort was impossible, observation of adjacent landforms and review of soil survey maps yielded some basic knowledge of the local soil profile. The Piedmont and Mountain regions of the southeast suffered extreme soil erosion and deflation in the nineteenth and twentieth centuries. In much of the survey area, gold mining in the aftermath of Removal resulted in massive colluviation of stream bottoms and springs. The combination of erosion, deflation, and colluviation resulted in the destruction and/or deep burial of many archaeological sites. Sites that were occupied only briefly (and thus would have left only a limited archaeological

signature to begin with) were especially vulnerable. We offer a potential mechanism for more-intensive archaeological surveys in the future in the section, Certification and Further Research.

In addition to this technical report, summary information and links to related websites can be found on the Georgia Trail of Tears initiative website at: . Finally, two tri-fold pamphlets that summarize the project and include a driving tour of the survey area are available from the Georgia Department of Natural Resources Historic Preservation Division, Office of the State Archaeologist, 47 Trinity Avenue SW, Atlanta, Georgia 30334.

The Cherokee Nation in Georgia

An Overview

In the late spring of 1836, when the U.S. Senate ratified the Treaty of New Echota, the Cherokee Nation in Georgia covered more than 6,000 square miles. Its western boundary abutted the present-day Alabama state line and its northern boundary formed the Tennessee state line. To the east and south, the Cherokee Nation was bounded by the Georgia counties of Rabun, Habersham, Hall, Gwinnett, Henry, Fayette, and Carroll (Illustration 1: Atlas: Cherokee Nation in Georgia). According to the 1835 Cherokee census, 8,936 Cherokees lived within the chartered limits of Georgia, along with 776 African-American slaves and 68 intermarried whites. [i]

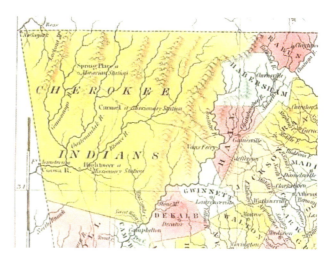

Illustration 1. The Cherokee Nation.

Physiography

The Cherokee Nation occupied the most complex geological region of Georgia, one that encompasses four of the state's five physiographic provinces: the Appalachian Plateau, Blue Ridge, Piedmont, and Ridge and Valley (Illustration 2: Ga Atlas Physiography).

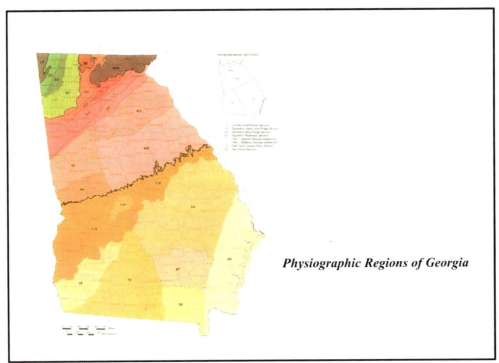

Illustration 2.   Physiography of Georgia.

The Appalachian Plateau lies in the extreme northwest corner of the state and is characterized by two sandstone-capped mountains that rise to 2,000 feet and are separated by a narrow valley underlain by limestone.[ii] Between the two mountains, Lookout Valley offered the best soils for Cherokee farming and gave access to forested areas with mast and game. Today Dade is the sole Georgia County located in the Appalachian province. Until 1939 Dade County could be entered by road only through Alabama or Tennessee. Georgia's 1939 purchase of Cloudland Canyon finally connected the county with the state of Georgia.

Adjacent to the Plateau, the **Ridge and Valley province** trends northeasterly with discontinuous valleys and relatively narrow, low ridges. The greatest elevation occurs in the chevron-shaped Armuchee Ridges that abruptly rise 600 to 700 feet.[iii] The present-day counties of Catoosa, Walker, and Chattooga occupy and extend beyond the Armuchee Ridges, with Walker occupying the greatest portion (Illustration 3: Ga counties). In general, the Ridge and Valley forests provided resources for food, tools, transportation, and housing.

East of the Armuchee ridges, the Great Valley opens with a few scattered hills and ridges rising 800 feet.[iv] Present-day counties in the Great Valley include all of Whitfield and Floyd, and the majority of Murray, Gordon, Bartow, and Polk (Illustration 3: Ga counties). Throughout the Ridge and Valley, soils composed of organic materials mixed with weathered rock detritus proved favorable for Cherokee agriculture and pasturage.

The eastern boundary of the Ridge and Valley adjoins both the Piedmont province and the **Blue Ridge province**, which includes irregular masses of rugged, heavily forested mountains, multiple streams, and valleys of varying widths and depths. The highest elevations in the Cherokee Nation in Georgia appeared in the Cohutta and Blue Ridge Mountains of the Blue

Ridge province, where ranges surpass 4,000 feet.[v] Cross ridges between the two ranges add to the region's physiographic and ecological complexity.

Illustration 3. Georgia Counties.

The Blue Ridge and Cohutta ranges form the Georgia portion of the Appalachian mountain chain. Few gaps in the Blue Ridge can be surmounted easily. Those most accessible are Rabun Gap with an elevation of 2,100 feet and Unicoi Gap, whose elevation is 2,900 feet.[vi] By the time of Cherokee removal, roads had been constructed across both. Portions of Fannin, Gilmer, and Murray counties lie in the Cohutta segment; Union, Towns, and most of Rabun are in the Blue Ridge Mountains (Illustration 3: Ga counties).

The remainder of the Cherokee Nation in Georgia lies in the three upland segments of the **Piedmont province**--Cherokee, Central, and Dahlonega--which today include all of Haralson, Douglas, Paulding, Cobb, Cherokee, and Forsyth counties, and considerable portions of Dawson, Pickens, Gilmer, and Lumpkin counties (Illustration 3: Ga counties).

Bounded by the fall line on the on the east and the mountains on the west, the upland Piedmont consists of predominantly rolling terrain dissected by relatively deep river valleys as well as minor streams and creeks. Its well-drained, reddish, clayey soils are underlain by granite and in Cherokee Georgia were often covered with lush vegetation.[vii] Stone outcrops and ridges rise from 100-1,000 feet above the general elevation, which reaches 1,500 feet above sea level.[viii]

The northern part of the Cherokee segment contains westward-flowing streams while the streams of the southern half flow southwestward. The northern Dahlonega is rough and hilly where streams flowing from the Blue Ridge have cut narrow valleys. The southern Dahlonega is flatter with correspondingly wider stream valleys. The Central Uplands form the broadest and longest segment of the Cherokee Piedmont, with low ridges and stream valleys ranging from broad and open to relatively narrow and shallow (Illustration 2: Ga Atlas Physiography).[ix]

Environment and Ecology

The Cherokees exploited their environment for food, water, medicines, tools, clothing, construction materials, and trade goods. Knowledge of vegetation as well as animals, insects, birds, reptiles, and amphibians was essential to their ability to create everything from wasp soup and bloodroot dye to sassafras tea and turtle-shell rattles. Even in the early nineteenth century when so much about their world was changing, Cherokees continued to gather foods, medicines, and materials from their local landscapes to survive and thrive. Understanding the impact of removal is scarcely possible without recognizing how Cherokees interacted with their environment.

Cherokee Georgia developed primarily in mixed deciduous and southern **Appalachian forests**, characterized by a preponderance of broad-leafed trees interspersed with pines, hemlocks, and magnolias. In these forests, dozens of tree species compete for light, space, water, and nutrients. They create a crowded canopy and understory, which in turn, give rise to vibrant forest floors and soils. Every leaf becomes a source of nutrients for something, whether microbial, vegetable, bird, or mammal. Supported by climate variations and abundant food supplies, numerous microhabitats co-exist in the same niches.

Chestnut, white oak, and hickory were the mainstays of the Cherokee forest and each was important in Cherokee life. In addition to sustaining the populations of numerous small mammals, chestnut was a favorite food for Cherokees, who spent winter evenings shelling them around a common fire. Women made enormous flat loaves of chestnut bread and wrapped individual servings in the shucks of

corn, a tradition that continues among the Cherokees of North Carolina. Public and private buildings and their roofs, as well as furniture, were made of white oak.

Cherokees who added puncheons to their cabin floors used oak, according to an anonymous writer who lived in the Nation from 1828-30. "Two new puncheons or planks," he wrote of the cabin he visited, "had been split from an oak log and brought to the house and laid down where the floor should be but no adze had passed over them. The sides were as smooth and as soft as when separated from the parent tree."[x] Tools such as the ubiquitous corn pounder were made of hickory. When mixed with cold water the nuts from hickory trees made "hickory milk," a rich and nourishing drink, and the combination of corn and hickory nuts produced a favorite food.[xi]

Variations in the chestnut-oak-hickory forests occurred in the different physiographic provinces. The Appalachian Plateau's oak-hickory forests nurtured sweet gum, yellow poplar, elm, and maple trees as well as white ash, shortleaf and loblolly pines.[xii] Poplar trunks became dugout canoes in the hands of the Cherokees. In the higher elevations of the Blue Ridge province, a much greater occurrence of chestnut could be found along with cherry, cucumber, and cottonwood.[xiii] To the west, vegetation of the equally high Dahlonega Plateau

Chestnut   *Oak*   *Hickory*

included Virginia pine, sweet gum, dogwood, mimosa, and black locust, this last making its southernmost appearance here.[xiv] In the Ridge and Valley, oak-pine forests were interspersed with the more abundant oak-hickory forests. At lower elevations loblolly-short leaf pine forests appeared.[xv] As many as 34 different kinds of trees grew in the oak-pine-hickory forests of the Cherokee Piedmont.[xvi] Deciduous trees included black cherry, red maple, winged elm, and sassafras.[xvii] As forests matured, different shrubs appeared such as arrowwood, wild azalea, blueberry, strawberry bush, and shadbush.[xviii]

Plant associations of the chestnut-oak-hickory composition include ash, yellow poplar, elm, and maple.[xix] The diversity created by climate and nutrients was and is most evident among understory plants. Dogwood, redbud, striped maple, sourwood, hophornbeam, mulberry, and various kinds of magnolia grow thickly, and they gave seasonal color, food, medicines, and manufacturing goods to the Cherokees. Beneath the understory, more vegetation appears such as spicebush, witch hazel, pawpaw, wild hydrangea, pepperbush, and Hercules club.[xx] The deciduous forest floor supports an extraordinary array of flower species from early spring ephemerals to late bloomers. Bloodroot, larkspur, phacelia, spring beauty, trillium, hepatica, violets, ginger, mint, wild potato (the name of a Cherokee clan), and lady's slipper, which Cherokees called "moccasin flower," appear on forest floors. In addition to serving as a medicinal, bloodroot provided women with a reddish dye for the hundreds of baskets they made and used in a lifetime. Even in the present, North Carolina Cherokees may use lady's slipper for heart ailments.

Trillium

Violet

Lady's Slipper

Bloodroot

The mixed deciduous forests are home to a variety of **mammals and birds**. Annually the forests produce thousands of pounds of dank and fragrant litter that give rise to mushrooms (a popular winter food among Cherokees), moss, lichens, and other vegetation. Cherokees gathered moss and lichens for added salt. Deer, bear, and turkey are the principal larger animals in deciduous forests but smaller animal life abounds. Reptiles, birds, butterflies, raccoons, fox, skunks, wasps, beaver, opossum, and woodchucks were familiar characters in Cherokee lore and important elements in Cherokee economy. By the early 1800s, the once-abundant populations of deer and turkey had dwindled dramatically from over hunting and loss of habitat to farms and pastures. The changing landscape contributed to the necessity for Cherokees to adopt the farming and market economy encouraged (if not required) by the federal government.

Other birds found in Cherokee Georgia included owls, hawks, ravens, and crows, all of which gave patronymics to Cherokee families and clans and filled their legends with warnings and hauntings. Quail, doves, ducks, wild geese, and ruffled grouse were among the game birds available to the native hunters, and numerous songbirds such as brown thrashers, indigo buntings, towhees, cardinals, robins, wrens, thrushes, and warblers nested in the forests.[xxi] Spring brought waves of migrants including the cuckoo, blue jay, warbler, king bird, barn swallow, and whippoorwill.[xxii] Cherokees used feathers from specific birds for amulets and ornamentation, gathered eggs for food, and roasted whole birds to supplement their diet.

Cherokee Georgia enjoyed four distinct **seasons** of approximate equal length. In midsummer, temperatures ranged from 60 to 90 degrees Fahrenheit, while midwinter ranged from 25 to 50 degrees Fahrenheit.[xxiii] Influenced by elevation, the average annual precipitation in the mountainous northeast was about 70 inches. [xxiv] Rainfall in the Piedmont was 40-50 inches per year distributed relatively evenly over the annual cycle.[xxv] With good drainage, northeastern soils eroded easily and were most useful for pasture and forests; soils to the northwest supported row crops.[xxvi] Growing season was longest in the Piedmont, lasting at least 180 days per year.[xxvii] As Cherokees began animal husbandry in the late eighteenth and early nineteenth centuries, they utilized and shaped a landscape suitable for herds of cattle, sheep, goats, pigs, and horses. Household gardens continued, almost always cultivated by the women, but men began farming on large cleared fields of as much as 10-15 acres.

Cherokees were never passive occupants of an unchanging environment. They regularly burned forests to clear litter and expose game; they cleared plots for farmland and gathered enormous quantities of nuts, fruits, roots, and wild plants, erected stone weirs in rivers and streams to trap fish, dug moats, and cut down trees to build homes and public buildings.

Changing Landscapes and Economies

The arrival of Europeans and their increasing encroachment, however, greatly accelerated the pace of environmental and economic change. By the 1830s, both Cherokees and whites farmed with plows, reducing priceless topsoil. European bounties on predator animals virtually eliminated the wolf, fox, panther, and mountain lion. The buffalo and elk had disappeared when guns became common in the eighteenth century. Road building interrupted game paths and caused runoff of rainwater and silting of streams. Population increases, both white and Cherokee, diminished game and nesting sites. Introduced plants and animals changed farming preferences, domestic architecture, settlement patterns, landscapes, and trade networks.

Domesticated animals including pigs, horses, cattle, goats, and sheep all required feeding and fencing. When freed to forage, they trampled and consumed native vegetation, eliminating plants such as river cane. By the 1830s, Cherokees in Georgia owned nearly 80,000 head of livestock, which necessitated thousands of pens and miles of fences.[xxviii] Blacksmith shops appeared in response to the demand for new farm tools and horse equipment such as shoes, nails, saddles, bridles, and wagon fittings.

The introduction of **northern European vegetables** extended agricultural seasons, and the introduction of cotton agriculture depleted soils while developing new markets. In 1826 John Ridge wrote that "cotton is generally raised for domestic consumption and a few have grown it for market and have realized very good profits."[xxix] Rising profits spurred the development of economic differentiation and by the 1830s, several Cherokees in Georgia--Major Ridge, John Ross, John Martin, Joseph Vann, and James Daniel, for example--were among the wealthiest in the Nation. Domestic consumption of cotton meant

that women were making use of the spinning wheels and cotton cards distributed by the federal government; and their use of government looms indicated the new importance of sheep in their economy.

Another important change in Cherokee ecology arrived with **domesticated fruit trees**. Cherokees incorporated peaches into their subsistence economy so rapidly that many whites and Natives assumed they were indigenous. The property valuations of 1836-37 enumerated nearly 80,000 fruit trees, 63,000 of which were peach. Nearly every Cherokee homestead grew peach trees, with apple following in popularity. In addition, they planted cherry, pear, quince, and plum trees.[xxx] By raising fruit trees, Cherokees diminished their reliance on native fruits such as pawpaw, persimmon, and mulberry. They fed excess fruit to their hogs and Cherokees traveling from one place to another continued the tradition of helping themselves to the bounty of fruit they found in their neighbors' orchards, a custom that greatly frustrated the missionaries who were unfamiliar with the custom.

Georgia Cherokees of the 1830s owned more than 6,000 **dwellings and out-buildings**.[xxxi] Their cabins, corn cribs, separate kitchens, smoke houses, potato houses, and, for some, slave cabins, were made of local timber, primarily the abundant white oak that had proven both malleable and durable. To meet the rising demand for planked wood, saw mills appeared on the rapidly-changing landscape. Whites and Cherokees also built grist mills on local streams and increasing numbers of Cherokees ground their corn rather than pounding it in the mortar as they had for generations. Other crops required grist mills as well. According to John Ridge, "wheat, rye, and oats grow very well and some families have commenced to introduce them on their farms."[xxxii]

The 1835 Cherokee census reveals that Georgia Cherokees cultivated nearly 20,000 acres and produced 269,000 bushels of corn, selling approximately one quarter of it. The following year they drove 40,000 hogs to middle Alabama and Georgia, where cotton production resulted in food scarcity.[xxxiii] The statistics reveal the extent to which Georgia Cherokees were successful in developing new economies in accord with their own preferences as well as with pressure for removal. The common complaint that Indians did not make productive use of their land was wholly inaccurate in Cherokee Georgia.

Roads and Trails

In the early 1800's, new roads through the Nation facilitated commerce as Cherokees entered a market economy; later in the century, the same roads facilitated Cherokee deportation. In the late spring of 1838, thousands of Cherokees were forcibly marched along roads leading from their settlements to nearby forts or encampments, then on to the New Echota headquarters of the Middle Military Command, or to Ft. Butler in North Carolina, Ross's Landing or Athens in Tennessee, or Ft. Payne,

Alabama. To expedite removal, all posts were positioned near major roads, which had to be sufficiently wide to accommodate wagons as well as horses and thousands of captives. All but one of the roads was in place by the time the Cherokees were expelled from Georgia.

By the mid-1830s, the Cherokee Nation in Georgia was crisscrossed with roads and trails utilized by everyone from pioneers and stock drivers to mail carriers and missionaries (Illustration 4: GA Trails and roads). In light of the complexity of the road and trail system in Cherokee Georgia, this report addresses only those likely to have been utilized in Cherokee removal. Some of the roads were constructed by the federal government, others by the state, and still others were public roads that were established over time as game trails, war paths, and trade paths.

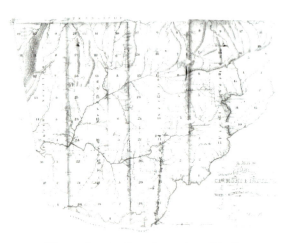

Illustration 4. Georgia roads and trails.

The Georgia or Federal Road

In 1803, the Secretary of War succeeded in persuading the Cherokee Nation to grant permission for a wagon road "not to exceed sixty feet in width" to originate at two sites on Cherokee land, Tellico and Southwest Point (later Kingston), Tennessee, and to run through the Cherokee Nation to the Georgia town of

Athens.[xxxiv] The purpose of the road was to connect dispersed white settlements, to provide Tennesseans access to southern markets at Augusta and Savannah, and to create entryways into the Cherokee Nation. Most of the Nation opposed road construction but by offering James Vann and other prominent Cherokees "a proper inducement," Agent Return Meigs gained their support for the road.[xxxv]

Cherokees reserved the right to control and receive revenue from all ferries and tolls, and to construct inns and public houses or stands along the road.[xxxvi] By the time of removal, a considerable number of Cherokees had become relatively wealthy from road-related businesses. Prominent among the entrepreneurs were those who had signed the road agreement: Charles Hicks, Pathkiller, James Vann, and Black Fox. Vann and Hicks resided in Cherokee Georgia.

According to the agreement "one ferry shall be kept at Southwest point, one at Tellico, and one at the river Chatahuchee where the said road shall cross the said river." In addition, "the Cherokee Nation shall establish houses of entertainment on the said road at three places to wit at Southwest point, Tellico, and Chatahuchee, at the ferries aforesaid."[xxxvii] Soon after, James Vann became the first ferry owner as well as the first owner of a public stop in Cherokee Georgia, both on the Federal Road at the Chattahoochee River (Illustration 5: Vann tavern).

An early traveler reminds us that ferries were still somewhat unusual. "In the course of two or three days, we came to a river, which was crossed by means of a ferry-boat, the first that I have ever seen. It was a broad, shallow, flat-bottomed thing, with a double floor built of very

Illustration 5. The Vann Tavern.

thick planks, having space enough for a large wagon and team, and making one think of an ordinary plank bridge turned bottom upwards. A rope of twisted hide was stretched across the river and fastened to a tree on each side. The flat was pulled across by means of this rope."[xxxviii]

Soon after the road agreement was signed, Col. William Barnett and Brig. Gen. Buckner Harris of Jackson County wrote to Tennessee governor John Sevier in their capacity as commissioners responsible for laying off the road. Presuming that the Secretary of War had informed Sevier of the appropriate procedures, Barnett and Harris proposed meeting the Tennessee commissioners at James Vann's house on August 15th.[xxxix] Sevier promptly agreed to the meeting and wrote Tennesseans Joseph McMinn, Samuel Wear, and John Cowan to attend.[xl] Work soon began surveying and building the federal road.

By February 1805, Agent Return Meigs faced an unexpected road problem. Apparently some Cherokees in Coosawattee erected their own turnpike gate and charged three white men for using the road. That month, Meigs reimbursed Samuel Jones, John Mote, and Francis Jones "for money extracted from them by Cherokee Indians at Coosawattee under a mistaken idea that they had the right to establish a turnpike gate and to receive toll on the road between Tennessee and Georgia." In August of the same year, he again had to pay an unsuspecting white man, one Joseph Nation, "for money extracted improperly at Koosotowee [sic] at a turnpike gate." The Coosawattee gatekeepers charged one additional person before disappearing from the record books. On Dec. 1, 1805, Meigs reimbursed William Bridges for his turnpike fee of $1.50.[xli]

In addition to Vann and the Coosawattee entrepreneurs, the other Georgia Cherokee to profit early and legally from the road agreement was Charles Hicks, who served as interpreter for the commissioners. Hicks' usual compensation was $75 per quarter. In addition, in 1804 he received $10 specifically for interpreting for the Tennessee commissioners.[xlii]

The route of the Federal Road generally followed the old Cherokee Middle Path across northern Georgia, running diagonally south and east from the Tennessee line to Vann's ferry on the Chattahoochee River (Illustration 6: Tanner 1834 map).[xliii] The east prong extended from the first site of Old Tellico, Tennessee almost due south to present-day Tennga, Cisco, Eton, and Chatsworth, and then to James Vann's house and the Spring Place Moravian mission (1805). Just south of the mission, the road joined its west prong, which entered Georgia's chartered limits at Rossville, heading east and south, then crossed Chickamauga and Coyehula Creeks, the Conasauga River, and continued to the Vann house.

From the Vann house, the now-single road crossed the Coosawattee River and went by the populous town of Coosawattee and the unexpected tollgate. Continuing south and east the road passed Taloney and the site of the Carmel mission (established 1819), ran past Talking Rock at Talking Rock Creek, and

Illustration 6. Tanner's 1834 map.

threaded between sites on Long Swamp Creek that became public stops at Ambrose Harnage's and James Daniel's in the present-day town of Tate. Harnage, with his Cherokee wife and African American slaves, lived on the south side of the road; on the north side Daniel lived as one of the wealthiest men in the Nation with 37 slaves, 30 houses, and 300 acres.[xliv]

After crossing the Etowah River at Frogtown or Blackburn's ford, the Federal Road intersected the Upper Alabama Road running due west. From the Etowah crossing the road passed by Jacob Scudder's home and stage stop, then continued to the upper Chattahoochee River where James Vann had established his ferry and public stop, and on beyond the Cherokee Nation's limits.

A white man, Scudder had no family connections in the Nation and was therefore required to pay business taxes. On Dec. 27, 1825, John Ross protested to agent Hugh Montgomery that Scudder, "under the garb of a licensed Trader, has for a considerable time past been engaged in keeping a house of entertainment at the forks of the Tennessee [Federal] and Alabama roads, east of the Hightower [Etowah] River, in opposition to and prejudicial to the interests of the Native Citizens occupying Stands near that place."[xlv] On behalf of the Cherokee National Council, Ross requested that Scudder and other intruders be removed. However, no action was taken by the government agents.

According to Marion Hemperley, former Surveyor General of Georgia, the road did not cross Talking Rock Creek. "as does Ga 136, but turned right along the foot of the mountain" at the Coosawattee town site.[xlvi] In 1842, however, the Georgia General Assembly incorporated the Talking Rock Turnpike Company with a provision to construct a turnpike "from the east bank of the Coosawattee River, in the county of Murray, just above the mouth of Talking Rock Creek, where the Federal Road now crosses said Creek."[xlvii] The Georgia Department of Transportation plans a complete survey of the Federal Road, to be completed by 2005. The results of the survey may settle the question of the possible passage at Talking Rock Creek.

Traveling on the Federal Road near Blackburn's in 1818, Ebenezer Newton (1790-1859) decried the poor condition of the road, which was described as "pretty rough" and getting worse just past the Chattahoochee River. After crossing the Etowah, his party had to travel slowly "owing to the exceeding badness of the road."[xlviii] Near Blackburn's ferry, Newton saw the grave of James Vann, who had been murdered (or executed according to clan law) at nearby Blackburn's Tavern and buried on a low hill beside the road. "We observed, by the roadside on an eminence," he wrote, "a tomb paled in and painted black with an inscription at the head, on a board, "Here lies the body of James Vann who departed this life Feb. 1809 age 43.""[xlix]

Born in North Carolina, Lewis Blackburn married Cherokee Mary Daniel and owned slaves, lands, and improvements on both sides of the Etowah River as well as the public ferry and stand at the Federal Road crossing. Blackburn's stand on the west side of the Etowah River was sufficiently well known to be utilized by President James Monroe and Secretary of War John C. Calhoun when they journeyed through the Cherokee Nation in 1819. When Cherokee improvements were evaluated in 1835, Blackburn's ferry was estimated to earn two hundred dollars per year.[l]

Initially called the Georgia Road, the Federal Road in the Cherokee Nation passed through the present-day counties of Catoosa, Whitfield, Murray, Gilmer, Pickens, Dawson, and Forsyth. Robert S. Davis, Jr. has written that the "trail usually followed the tops of ridges and hills, only coming down to the bottoms when it was necessary to go from one ridge to the other."[li]

In 1838 four military posts were established on or very near the Federal Road: Ft. Hoskins and Ft. Gilmer (Murray County), Ft. Newnan (near George Sanders' and Talking Rock), and Ft. Campbell near Scudder's (Forsyth County). The road gave the militia access to the internment camps that were established in Tennessee.

Postal Roads

At the two 1805 Tellico Treaties, the Cherokees ceded additional land and consented to the free use by American citizens of two additional roads for mail service. One would be established from Franklin (Tennessee) to settlements on the Tombigbee River (Alabama) and a second from the head of Stone's River in Tennessee (near Murfreesboro) to "a suitable place towards the southern frontier of the Cherokees."[lii] The first mail road lay beyond the limits of Cherokee Georgia; it is likely the second created an opening in the Cedar Town area since that was the southern terminus of the Nation in 1805. Additional research may provide information about the second postal road. Meanwhile we can be certain the establishment of a postal road into the Nation increased the likelihood of white encroachment.

In the absence of relevant maps, we can infer postal roads by identifying postmasters. In 1827 the trader Jacob Scudder was postmaster at Hightower and missionary Samuel Worcester held the same position at Spring Place or New Echota. William J. Tarvin, and Moravian missionaries Gottlieb Byhan and Henry G. Clauder also served as postmasters at Spring Place. The mailing address on a letter from Gov. Wilson Lumpkin to Col. C.H. Nelson, dated Jan. 12, 1835, is Long Swamp Post Office.[liii] Long Swamp was a Cherokee settlement on Long Swamp Creek in present-day Pickens County. No information has been found to identify a possible post office at Long Swamp.

The Unicoi Turnpike

In 1813, Cherokees consented to the establishment of a turnpike road from the Tugaloo to the Chattahoochee Rivers. The route followed an old and well-traversed Indian trail that connected Cherokee towns in Georgia and North Carolina. The federal government gained Cherokee approval for the road and authorized the establishment of a turnpike company to run to road and pay a fee of $160 per annum to the Nation for twenty years. Georgia passed

authorizing legislation in 1816 and the road was completed by 1819.[liv] As its historical marker reads, the road was "the first vehicular road to link eastern Tennessee, western North Carolina, and north Georgia with the head of navigation on the Savannah River system." The turnpike began on the Tugaloo River east of Toccoa and led through Unicoi Gap in the Blue Ridge Mountains, at 3,000 feet the lowest elevation in the chain. From the eastern part of Union County, the road traveled to Murphy, North Carolina, then on to Nine Mile Creek in Tennessee.

In anticipation of the 1838 removal, Ft. Hetzel was established in Ellijay and a military encampment was proposed for Union County "near Chastain's." Commanders of both posts were to report to the headquarters of the Eastern Command at Ft. Butler in Murphy, North Carolina. Cherokees from Ellijay and Union County were rounded up by the militias and marched along the Unicoi Turnpike to Ft. Butler, and then on to the internment camps in Tennessee.

The Alabama Roads

A series of east-west trails, all called the Alabama Road, crossed the Cherokee Nation in Georgia and led to the Alabama Territory from Georgia, Tennessee, and the Carolinas (Illustration 6: 1834 Tanner map). Inasmuch as sections of the Old Alabama Road remain intact, it would be appropriate to place Trail of Tears signage at locations near the now-inundated site of Sixes and the site of Ft. Buffington.

In Cherokee Georgia, the **Upper Alabama Road** dropped southward from Leather's Ford on the Chestatee River (Lumpkin County) and followed the north side of the Etowah River in Dawson County, past Tensawattee or Big Savannah (later Dougherty), then dropped to the south side of the river in Forsyth County where it crossed the Federal Road at Jacob Scudder's home and stand at Hightower crossroads.

Continuing west-southwest on the south side of the river, the Alabama Road ran through Cherokee County almost to the town of Sixes. It crossed again to the north side near Moses Downing's ferry (Illustration 7: 1846 Mitchell map Cherokee county). From the east to this point, it is also known as the Downing Ferry Road. Moses Downing was a prosperous Cherokee of white and Cherokee ancestry. In addition to a ferry, he owned 115 acres of Etowah bottomlands, 11 houses, and 5 slaves.[lv] With proximity to large Cherokee towns in the Etowah valley, his ferry crossing was doubtless well traveled and often used.

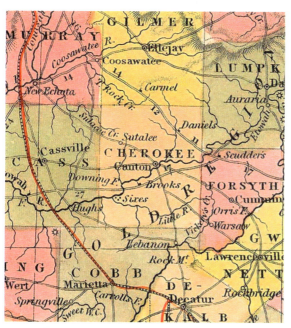

Illustration 7. Cherokee County in 1846.

From Downing's ferry, the road traveled slightly north and nearly due west through somewhat rugged terrain near Lick Creek. West of the creek it forked at the site of Hawk's store (now Cass Station).[lvi] On the north side of the

river, the upper fork trended northward to Cass (now Bartow) County. Hemperley stated that it ran by the Etowah or Hightower mission site (founded 1822) on Pumpkinvine Creek (Illustration 8: 1834 map Cherokee County).[lvii] North of the creek and river stood the great Etowah mounds, remnants of the Mississippian peoples who preceded the Cherokees. The upper fork, by now referred to as the Upper Alabama Road, led on to Floyd County and Ridge's ferry on the Oostanaula River, then crossed the river and continued westward to the Alabama Territory.

Illustration 8. An 1834 map of Cherokee County.

The lower fork, hereafter called the Lower Alabama Road, crossed to the south side of the Etowah River and ran to a public stop owned by a white man, Jacob West. West's station stood at a crossroads formed by the Lower Alabama's intersection with a north-south road that led to the point where the Etowah River joined the Oostanaula. John Ross'ss ferry, formerly owned by Widow Fool, operated at that junction.[lviii]

From a southerly direction, the **Lower Alabama Road** entered the Cherokee Nation on the west side of the Chattahoochee River at a ferry crossing owned by George Waters, a wealthy Cherokee of mixed parentage. Waters owned 300 acres and 2 farms, as well as 100 black slaves.[lix] His name survives in corrupted form as Warsaw and identifies a present-day community at the Forsyth County site.

Heading west-northwest, the road entered Cherokee County and was joined by a trail variously called the Shallow Ford or Bell's Ferry Road. Continuing on into Cass (now Bartow) County, the now-merged road crossed Allatoona Creek, a tributary of the Etowah, and led northward to the Etowah at the Hughes ferry crossing. Just northwest of the crossing it intersected the lower fork of the Upper Alabama Road and is thus hereafter called the Lower Alabama. Turning south and west, it entered Vann's Valley near Cave Spring, crossed Cedar Creek and entered Cedar Town before leading to Alabama (Illustration 9: Mitchell map 1846 Paulding County)[lx].

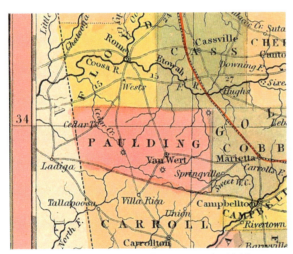

Illustration 9. Paulding County in 1846.

In 1838 the Upper and Lower Alabama roads connected Ft. Buffington and the encampment at Sixes (both in Cherokee County) with posts to the east on the Federal Road and with those to the west at Rome. Trail of Tears signage could be considered at several locations.

Alabama Road North-South Connectors

Two north-south trails connected the east-west Alabama roads with important sites. The westernmost trail led from West's to the forks of the Oostanaula and Etowah rivers (at Ross's ferry) and headed north and slightly east to Coosawattee on the Federal Road. Also called the Alabama Road, it linked the two east-west forks with one another and the Federal Road.

East and nearly parallel to it, the Sally Hughes Road ran from her ferry crossing on the Etowah River, along the east side of Pine Log Creek, and north to New Echota. Just as New Echota was often called New Town, the Sally Hughes Road was often referred to as the New Town Road (Illustration 6: 1834 Tanner map). From New Echota north, the road is sometimes called the Tennessee Road.[lxi]

An indication of the rapidity of road and ferry building in the Nation can be seen in an 1832 complaint Sally Hughes made to the governor of Georgia that John Dawson and Jesse Day had "turn'd the public road at least one half mile above where the road lately cRoss'sd [sic] the Etowah River and have erected a ferry…to the prejudice of the Indians." No records have appeared indicating that Hughes received satisfaction from the state regarding her competitor's roadway and ferry. When surveyors assessed the Hughes ferry in 1832, Dawson claimed to own it.[lxii]

In 1838, the north-south connectors of the Alabama Roads linked the posts at Rome--Camp Scott and Ft. Means (Floyd County)--to one another and to Ft. Wool at New Echota (Murray County). A line in the "Memoranda of Routes in the Cherokee Country" states "to Ft. Buffington, passes near the Sixes," which appears to refer to the route from New Echota. The memorandum also indicates that the westernmost connector from West's also extended southward to

Cedar Town in Paulding County (Illustration 9: 1846 Mitchell Paulding County).[lxiii]

The Brainerd Roads

To the north, two so-called Alabama Roads led from the mission station at Brainerd, Tennessee (founded 1818) across the northwestern tip of Georgia's chartered limits to northern Alabama and to Rome in Floyd County. They are sometimes referred to as Brainerd roads and doubtless saw considerable traffic after the mission was opened.

The east road came from Calhoun, Tennessee, site of the Cherokee Agency, and crossed the present-day state line above Ringgold before joining the Federal Road. The west road entered Georgia's limits at present-day Graysville in Catoosa County and then intersected the Federal Road.

From the Federal Road, the two ran as one through most of Walker County, passing to the east side of Lafayette, then splitting to run on either side of the Chattooga River. The west fork entered north central Alabama while the east fork came to the east side of the Chattooga river, the west side of Armuchee Creek, then crossed the Etowah River and intersected the Upper Alabama Road in Floyd County[lxiv] (Illustration 10: 1839 Burr map of Walker County).

In 1838, the Brainerd roads connected Ft. Cumming (Walker County) with the collection depot at Ross's Landing and Ft. Cass, Tennessee, and with the southerly posts at Rome, which then accessed Ft. Wool at New Echota. The 1838 "memoranda of Routes in the

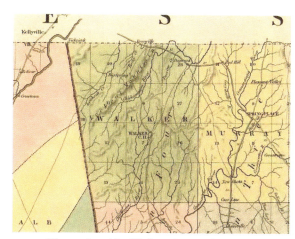

Illustration 10. Walker County in 1839.

Cherokee Country" designates a route from Ft. Cass "at Ross's Landing to Fort Cumming, Georgia."[lxv]

Following the deportation of Georgia Cherokees, Brainerd mission became a way station for the dispossessed. On Thursday, May 21, 1838, for example, missionary Daniel Butrick wrote in his Brainerd diary that a young lieutenant had come to request camping permission for some Cherokees. Assenting, Butrick was astonished to see "a company of about two hundred Cherokees" driven onto the mission grounds. The following day they were forced "on to the camps 2.5 miles from the mission."[lxvi]

Dahlonega to the Federal Road

In 1834, the Georgia General Assembly established the Ellijay Turnpike Company with authority to open a wagon road "at least twenty feet wide" from Dahlonega (Lumpkin County) to Ellijay (Gilmer County) and from Ellijay to Tennessee, intersecting the Federal Road near its entry into Georgia's chartered limits. The company was further authorized to erect two toll-gates in Gilmer County but prohibited from charging Gilmer citizens for passage.[lxvii]

Presumably the Ellijay Turnpike Company did not succeed, for two years later the General Assembly appropriated ten thousand dollars for laying out a road from Dahlonega northwest to Ellijay and from Ellijay southwest to the Federal Road. The act stipulated that the road enter the Federal Road between Sumach Creek and the Coosawattee River.[lxviii] When finished, the route followed Cartecay Creek on the south side and entered the Federal Road at Talking Rock, a Cherokee settlement on Talking Rock Creek (Illustration 10: Burr map 1839). The 1837 Assembly records refer to the road as "nearly completed."[lxix] It was likely ready for the 1838 opening of the Dahlonega branch of the U.S. mint.

Trail of Tears signage could make use of the 1808 Georgia road law that directed all proprietors of toll bridges, ferries, and turnpike roads to "fix a board in a conspicuous situation...the Board to be painted Black with white characters...noting the rates of Toll or Ferriage."[lxx]

According to the 1836 General Assembly Acts, overseers of Georgia roads were required to open their roads at least thirty feet wide. An exception was made for the "new and sparsely populated" Union County where roads were required to be twenty feet wide with *twelve-foot causeways.[lxxi] Road width became particularly important during the removal of Cherokees. Military posts sent and received wagonloads of camp and garrison supplies, requiring roads adequately wide and well maintained. When removal actually took place, those Cherokees who were ill, elderly, or quite young were to be transported by wagon along with everyone's belongings.

During removal, the Federal Road from Dahlonega to Ellijay provided passage of camp and garrison supplies, including food and forage, from Ft. Floyd (Dahlonega) to Ft. Hetzel (Ellijay) and Ft. Newnan (Talking Rock). This was expedient because the quartermaster at Ft. Floyd had charge of the quartermaster supplies for the other three posts and those roads were particularly well traveled. The 1838 "Memoranda of Routes in the Cherokee Country" indicates the route from Ft. Hetzel to Dahlonega.[lxxii]

Tennessee to Hightower River Turnpike

1834 was the year for turnpikes, at least in the minds of Georgia General Assembly members. In addition to the Dahlonega road, the legislature established the Western Turnpike Company for a road from the Tennessee boundary and the Federal Road to the east bank of the Hightower (Etowah) River. The road was to be twenty feet wide and well maintained by the company.

Since instructions for the route do not indicate any deviation from the Federal Road itself, we might assume the turnpike anticipated the extinction of Cherokee land claims and also ensured the upkeep of the Federal Road from Tennessee at least as far as Scudder's at the Etowah River.

Auraria to Northern Boundary Line of Georgia

The legislature also incorporated the Auraria Blue Ridge Turnpike Company in 1834 for the construction of a turnpike running from the new gold mining town of Auraria (Lumpkin County) to a point on the northern boundary line of the state near Athens, Tennessee. Athens (McMinn County) was on "Eastinaula Creek" in southeast Tennessee, west of the Ocoee River and south of the Hiwassee.

No road appears to have followed a direct route from Auraria northwest to Athens, but the Blue Ridge Turnpike road connected Auraria to Dahlonega and possibly gave rise to the establishment of a station, or stop, which subsequently was interpreted as the site of Ft. Floyd. In 1954, the Georgia Historical Commission erected a bronze marker at the site of "The Station," interpreting the site as that of a removal stockade. Subsequent narratives and local informants embraced the notion that the marker commemorated "Ft. Dahlonega," and the damaged or stolen marker has been replaced twice (1997 and 1999). Research for this project has produced evidence that a removal fort called Ft. Floyd was established in Dahlonega close to the site of the U.S. Mint (now the grounds of North Georgia College and University). No documentation has been found to link "The Station" site with Ft. Floyd. No information been found that identifies the specific kind of station that was located near Auraria. Further research is planned.

The Laudsville to Blairsville Road

The 1834 incorporation act for the Auraria Blue Ridge Company included the additional incorporation of the Union Turnpike Company. It authorized construction of a turnpike road "from Laudsville, in Habersham County, through Tesintee Gap on the Blue Ridge, by the way of Blairsville, to some eligible point on the northern boundary of this state, in a direction towards the Tellico Plains in the state of Tennessee."[lxxiii] By 1836 the proposed route had proved sufficiently important for the legislature to appropriate money "to open and improve" the road. Apparently there had not been a sufficient number of Georgians living in

Union County in 1834 to construct and maintain the "best and nearest route from the Gold region of Georgia to East Tennessee."[lxxiv] A road to Blairsville and to the top of the Blue Ridge, however, likely gave further initiative for military posts to be established in the northeastern part of Cherokee Georgia at the time of removal.

North Carolina to Clarkesville

An approved draft of the 1836 legislative acts authorized money for the improvement of "the road from the line of North Carolina, in the Tennessee Valley; on through the Rabun Gap; on by way of Clayton; thence, on by way of the bridge on Tallula River, near Crane's ford, in Rabun County; thence on to Clarksville"[lxxv] (Illustration 11:1846 Mitchell map Habersham County).

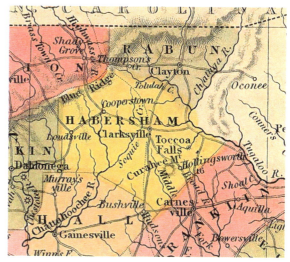

Illustration 11. Habersham County in 1846.

To the North Carolina Line

The following year the General Assembly appointed commissioners for a road from Augusta to Clarkesville and a road "from the top of the Blue Ridge, down the Highwassee River, to the North Carolina line."[lxxvi] In spite of the mountainous terrain, road builders had finally connected northeast Georgia with the state of North Carolina.

In 1838, the military companies stationed in the northeastern part of Cherokee Georgia marched their captives to Ft. Butler in North Carolina, headquarters of the Eastern Military District. In addition to the troops encamped at Chastain's near Blairsville in Union County, the commanding officer at Ft. Hetzel in Ellijay (Gilmer County) reported to Gen. Eustis at Ft. Butler rather than to Gen. Floyd, commander of the Middle Military District. The 1838 "Memoranda of Routes in the Cherokee Country" includes the route from Ft. Hetzel to Chastain's and Ft. Butler.[lxxvii]

Research in the Georgia and Cherokee records indicates a flurry of road building in the two to three years prior to the removal of Cherokees. Factors influencing construction included the 1838 opening of the U.S. Mint in Dahlonega, the influx of settlers into Cherokee Georgia following the signing of the New Echota treaty, the increased need for stage and post roads, and the anticipation of Indian removal and the opening of Cherokee land for complete settlement. A May 1838 memoranda of "Stages from Gainesville" indicates travel of twelve to twenty miles per day, with no route specified.[lxxviii] The existence of the memorandum makes clear, however, that stages ran regularly into the Cherokee country, possibly utilizing roads not identified by this phase of research.

New Road Cut by Removal Troops

The militia cut one road in Cherokee Georgia. On March 27, 1838, Assistant Quartermaster J.J. Field at Ft. Hetzel wrote to Quartermaster A.R. Hetzel in Tennessee, "I have opened a road from Coosawattee to this place so wagons can come by here by way of Sanders [Ft. Newnan, Talking Rock]."[lxxix] Adding this notation to the road and trail information above, the lines in Lt. Keyes' map that connect all the posts in Georgia can be understood as relatively specific and accurate.

Cherokee Removal in Georgia

Georgia took the lead among states favoring the removal of Indians. In 1802, Georgia gave its lands west of the Chattahoochee River to the federal government in return for the government's pledge to remove all Indians from the state's chartered limits as soon as it could be done practicably and peacefully. Thenceforth Georgia demanded Indian expulsion.

In 1826, Wilson Lumpkin was elected to the House of Representatives and appointed to the Committee on Indian Affairs. He introduced a resolution to examine the possibility of Indian removal, and money was appropriated for commissioners to explore a suitable location west of the Mississippi River. Subsequently the commissioners reported favorably, and Lumpkin was reelected to Congress the same year Andrew Jackson was elected president on a platform of Indian removal. The Indian Removal bill emerged from the Indian Committee and was approved by the House of Representatives May 28, 1830.

From 1830-1835, removal treaties were signed with the Choctaws, Chickasaws, Seminoles, and Creeks. Eager to force the issue, particularly after gold was discovered in Cherokee Georgia, the state extended its laws over the Cherokee Nation, surveyed all Cherokee lands, and distributed them by lottery to its citizens. In 1830, Gov. George Gilmer requested federal troops to protect the gold mines that had been opened on Cherokee land. Representing the first military occupation of Cherokee Georgia, the federal troops were replaced in 1831 by the Georgia Guard, commanded by Col. W. A. Sanford and Col. Charles H. Nelson. The post stood east of Scudder's trade store and public stop at the crossing of the Alabama Road and the Federal Road, in present-day Forsyth County. Known as Camp Eaton under federal occupancy, the post was called Camp Gilmer when the Georgia Guard assumed command.

Other sites in the Cherokee Nation underwent significant changes about the same time. During the period in which the Georgia Guard replaced the federal soldiers at Scudder's, President Jackson appointed Benjamin F. Currey as Cherokee enrolling agent with headquarters at New Echota. In 1834, the Georgia General Assembly passed a joint resolution calling for the state militia to protect Georgia citizens and pro-removal Indians. Wilson Lumpkin, who was by then the governor, directed Col. William Bishop to command such a force, "not to exceed forty men." Bishop was authorized to construct barracks for his men and a suitable place for deposit of their supplies at his headquarters at Spring Place, site of the former Moravian mission.[lxxx] Militia Gen. Charles E. Nelson established Camp Scott at an unknown location in Rome for the same purpose. Other than New Echota, whose history is documented in this report, it remains unknown whether the various lots, offices, military posts, and buildings of the early 1830s were reused during removal. It is

likely Camp Scott was reused because the name remains unchanged throughout the study period.

In December, 1835, a group of Cherokees led by John Ridge, Elias Boudinot, and Major Ridge and known as the Treaty Party, met treaty commissioners at New Echota and signed a treaty relinquishing all southeastern Cherokee land (Illustration 12. Portraits of John Ridge, Elias Boudinot, and Major Ridge). The time of removal was set for two years hence, and the Georgia legislature decreed that all Indian occupancy would be invalid on May 25, 1838.

Illustration 12. John Ridge, Elias Boudinot, Major Ridge.

New Echota, former capitol of the Cherokee Nation, continued as headquarters for Cherokee enrollment and became the site where claims commissioners paid Cherokees for improvements and spoliations. Rations were also distributed at New Echota "for poor Cherokees." The commissioner representing Georgia was Wilson Lumpkin, former representative and governor. He arrived at New Echota in September 1836 and remained in office until late October 1837. Lumpkin's occupancy overlapped that of U.S. Gen. John Wool, who took command of the Army of East Tennessee and the Cherokee Nation in the summer of 1836, and moved to New Echota until the summer of 1837. Wool authorized construction of the first military buildings in Georgia directly associated with removal. In 1837, Col. William Lindsay replaced Gen. Wool and made Ft. Wool, as it was now called, the military headquarters for imminent Cherokee emigration.

By 1838, the headquarters for Cherokee removal had been moved to Ft. Cass, Tennessee, and Ft. Wool became the headquarters of the Middle Military District and the center of removal operations in Georgia. Col. Lindsay and Gov. Gilmer worked in concert to establish 14 additional posts in Georgia 10-20 miles apart and with access to major roads. The posts were never intended to house captive Indians but to provide shelter for troops and supplies as well as reassurance to Georgians.

Ten posts were fortified: Cumming in Walker County, Campbell in Forsyth County, Buffington in Cherokee County, Floyd in Lumpkin County, Gilmer and Hoskins in Murray County, Hetzel in Gilmer County, Means in Floyd County, Newnan in Pickens County, and Wool in Gordon County. Officers at four posts were assigned certain duties for nearby stations, which likely meant their own facilities were larger or had greater storage facilities. The quartermaster at Ft. Hoskins was responsible for medicines and hospital supplies for several stations. Two posts--Ft. Buffington and what became Ft. Floyd--were occupied by the fall of 1837 and were repositories for munitions distributed to other stations. The Ft. Floyd quartermaster was responsible for quartermaster departments at four additional posts. Ft. Wool's quartermaster oversaw supplies for four additional stations. Substantial storage facilities would have been necessary at each.

Five posts remained unfortified: Chastain's in Towns County (formerly Union), Cedar Town in Polk County (formerly Paulding), Sixes in Cherokee County, Camp Scott at Rome in Floyd County, and Perkins in Dade County. Chastain's and Ft. Hetzel were assigned to the Eastern Military District in North Carolina, although many of their reports were sent to Ft. Wool. Assigned to the Western Military District in Alabama, Camp Perkins was never manned except by a quartermaster who was stationed there for one week. He reported directly to the quartermaster at headquarters in Tennessee.

Virtually all troops in Georgia were state militia rather than U.S. forces, and virtually all posts in Georgia were occupied by Georgians. Each post was manned by at least one company of approximately 60 men, five to six officers, a wagon master, a physician, and a quartermaster. Five companies were sent to the encampment at Sixes, the greatest number assigned anywhere at one time. Mounted companies occupied most forts, which would have necessitated the construction of stables for horses and possibly a forge for horseshoes. Documents also record orders for the construction of storehouses, pickets, blockhouses, ovens, hospitals, and offices, and the distribution of muskets, pistols, scabbards, swords, powder, mess pans, nails, cook pots, iron, stationery, rations, and thousands of bushels of corn and bundles of fodder. Trees would have been cleared for a considerable distance and used for construction and fuel. Given the amount of clearing, soil disturbance, and construction, the likelihood of recovering information with archaeology is substantially greater than was assumed at the beginning of this study.

On May 24, 1838, Ga. Militia Gen. Charles Floyd arrived at Ft. Wool to take command of the Middle Military District. A West Point graduate and seasoned soldier, Floyd maintained strict control of Georgia forces. He required weekly written accounts and reported on an almost-daily basis to Gen. Winfield Scott in Tennessee. Each post commander submitted an estimate of the number of Indians within a ten-mile radius of his post and Floyd ordered commanders to arrest all Cherokees in their areas and immediately transport them to the nearest fortified station until a sufficient number had been collected to drive on to Ross's Landing. Each post retained at least one wagon and wagon master to assist in the transport. Due to Floyd's orders and the responses of those under his command, we have heretofore unknown details about the number of Indians arrested and sent to other states.

On May 26, Floyd himself led the first operation. Within a matter of days, several thousand Cherokees had been rounded up and marched to Ross's Landing. The greatest number, 950, came from Sixes and the smallest, 70, from Camp Scott in Rome. By June 15, Floyd reported to Gen Scott that no Indians were left in Georgia, and by the end of July the companies of Georgia militia had been mustered out. Indian removal from Georgia had been accomplished in 20 days.

The following discussion of the removal forts and stations in Georgia addresses location, appearance, occupation, and service. While a general chronological order prevails, forts that were linked in service or command appear together. The research over a two-to-three year period has positively identified the posts established in Georgia, at least one of which was entirely unknown (Camp Perkins in Dade County), has determined the number that were fortified (ten), has positively identified the counties, names, and commanders, the length of occupation, the minimum amount of supplies and activities, and heretofore unknown relationships between the posts. As of this writing, no documents have been found that

specify the exact site of any removal posts in Georgia. Archaeology remains the best avenue for positive identification.

A site report for each post follows this narrative, with copies of original and secondary documents attached to each. In addition, a chronology for each post has been compiled and supplements the site report and narrative.

Forts and Stations

Fort Wool

To this point, two repositories have proven particularly fruitful in the search for information about Ft. Wool: the New York State Library, which houses the collected papers of Gen. Wool, and the National Archives in Washington, D.C., which stores the reports of the United States quartermasters. No single repository has been found that contains the papers of Gen. Winfield Scott or of Gen. Eustis in North Carolina; nor have any collections surfaced that contain records of the officers serving at the various posts in Georgia and reporting to Scott, Floyd, or Eustis. While this narrative makes extensive use of the letter sent by Gen. Wool, no comparable collection of letters received by Wool or any other commander has been found. Charles Floyd's diary, located in the Georgia Historical Society, Savannah, scarcely refers to his work as commander at Ft. Wool. No document has been found that proposes or designates the location of the removal posts in Georgia or the individual authorized to make that decision. Research continues in an effort to fill in the many blank pages in the history of Cherokee removal from Georgia. New information will be added to this narrative and to the site forms as it becomes available.

The Military Occupation. Ft. Wool was located at New Echota on the Federal Road in present-day Gordon County. The occupation of New Echota had apparently continued uninterrupted from the time Cherokees established their capital, courthouse, council house, printing press, mission station/school, stores, and residences around 1818, until the military abandoned its headquarters and the property was taken over by winners of the state lottery in the late summer, 1838. The numbers of people living at New Echota dramatically increased during the removal period, particularly as Ft. Wool became the headquarters for the Middle Military District.

Cherokees lived at New Echota as late as 1837. The Cherokee National Committee, which included New Echotan Elias Boudinot, met with state commissioners and a likely site was one of the public buildings at New Echota. In June 1837, Boudinot and his family emigrated with John Ridge's party. Other well-known residents such as missionary Samuel Worcester had already left. In the fall of 1836, however, Cherokees were still using the council house for church and other gatherings.[lxxxi]

In July 1836, new occupiers arrived. From his headquarters in Athens, Tennessee, Gen. John E. Wool ordered Capt. Vernon of the East Tennessee Volunteers to march to and select a suitable encampment at New Echota.[lxxxii] The location of his campsite has not been determined. In accord with the treaty provisions, an agent was appointed to distribute rations to the indigent Cherokees and rations were also provided for the troops.[lxxxiii] Also in July, former governor Wilson Lumpkin received a letter from President Jackson appointing him commissioner to examine all Cherokee claims and perform all duties pertaining to the office. He and his secretary, Col. William H. Jackson, arrived at New Echota in September.[lxxxiv] Later, they were joined by Commissioner John Kennedy. To pay the claims they approved, the commissioners ordered the delivery of thousands of dollars, which came under military guard down the Federal Road from Athens, Tennessee. It is hard to imagine the removal military, former Georgia governor, claims commissioners, and displaced Cherokees living together in the most difficult period of Cherokee history.

Construction. Lumpkin's record of his work as commissioner contains useful information about the appearance of New Echota. In a letter to Lewis Cass, dated Sept. 9, 1836, Lumpkin wrote that repairs to the dilapidated buildings would be necessary in order to transact business.[lxxxv] The first military construction work (Oct.-Nov. 1836), undertaken at the order of Gen. Wool, was a reframing of the provision house intended for food that was to be distributed to "poor Cherokees."[lxxxvi] In December an additional provision house was constructed, complete with a "hasp and steeple" for the door. Tools, hardware, and supplies for the provision houses--such as handsaws, augers, chisels, pad locks, measures, weights, ink bottles, butcher knives, ropes, books, and quires of paper--would have necessitated additional storage facilities and would likely have left archaeological traces.[lxxxvii]

Over the next few months, orders went out from Gen. Wool for thousands of pounds of beef, bacon, pork, and flour for troops and Cherokees, and for thousands of blankets and items of clothing for Cherokees. The literal business of removal surely proved profitable for some as loaded wagons traveled to New Echota, Coosawattee, and Blackburn's Station (on the Federal Road in Forsyth County) with goods purchased from as near as next door and as far as New York. Interestingly, members of the Treaty Party such as Elias Boudinot and John Ridge were among those who sold food to the military for distribution to poor Cherokees.[lxxxviii] In November, Lt. Chas Hoskins was assigned to New Echota to take charge of the commissary, which was increasing in size and importance every day.[lxxxix]

In late 1836 and through 1837, numerous militia companies encamped at New Echota, but the first assigned and ordered to construct quarters was the company of Capt. William E. Derrick (ordered into service Nov. 14, 1836), followed soon after by Capt. Ezekial Buffington's company (ordered into service Dec. 10, 1836).[xc] Both companies were raised from the Georgia militia. Since their winter barracks consisted of floored huts with officers' quarters on the wings, they might have left archaeological traces as well as some of the hardware used in construction. By the beginning of 1837, orders had also been given for the erection of stables and an office for headquarters, this last to be constructed from council house materials. Hinges, locks, nails, and similar materials might still be discernible in the ground. The countryside around New Echota was rapidly being depleted of all supplies, making the post there the most expensive in the Army of the Cherokee Nation.[xci]

Commissioner Lumpkin and Gen. Wool found themselves in conflict over matters of authority, which perhaps accounts for the fact that Lumpkin seemed uncertain any repairs to the public buildings had been made.[xcii] By the end of January, however, military supplies must surely have warranted more construction or, at least, the full use of many surviving buildings. Orders went out for tens of thousands of musket cartridges and flints since all privates were to be furnished with arms, including pistols, pouches,

and horns, as well as mess kits, tents, camp kettles, and monthly food rations. At least one hundred pounds of iron was ordered for horseshoes, indicating the presence of a blacksmith, whose shop could possibly be located archaeologically.[xciii]

Militia Appearance. The clothing of the militia and regular army officers apparently differed considerably. While the regular army unquestionably wore standard uniforms, the militia seemed to lack them. Orders were given for each officer, non-commissioned officer, musician, and private to be comfortably clothed with at least one pair of good strong [?] shoes, two pairs of stockings, two pairs of pantaloons, a vest, two shirts, a coat, a stock, an overcoat, a blanket, and a decent hat or cap.[xciv] At one point, Gen. Wool expressed concern that the soldiers were too thinly clad for winter. More research on this question should prove fruitful and can provide us with an image of militia appearance.

Activities. In February 1837 a Cherokee council held at New Echota for the distribution of annuity monies included more than one thousand people. Most Cherokees (1,269) attending the meeting voted for the money to be deposited with the second principal chief, who was strongly opposed to the treaty, rather than with the National Committee, comprised of members of the Treaty Party. Gen. Wool was sufficiently sobered by their vote, as well as by their resistance to the New Echota Treaty, to earnestly request the addition of a full regiment of U.S. Infantry.[xcv] He repeatedly wrote that the Cherokees were opposed to the treaty and remained unwilling to move. No written record has emerged to indicate where the thousands of Cherokees camped, ate, or assembled for the council or even for the distribution of rations, but the numbers of individuals camping on the grounds gives a sense of the scale and scope of activity at the old Cherokee capital.

Apparently New Echota remained unfortified as late as September 1837, and at that time Lumpkin considered the idea of fortifications "silly." He claimed that no fortifications would ever be necessary at New Echota, as proposed by military leaders, and if at all necessary would be so only in places where the women and children of Georgia resided.[xcvi] Lumpkin's dismissal of the idea of fortifications eight months before removal began underscores the speed with which preparations proceeded the following spring. New Echota was fortified by March 1, 1838 and soon after the post was called Ft. Wool.[xcvii]

Commanders. Troops stationed at New Echota served under numerous commanders. Gen. Wool traveled frequently, often through the Cherokee Nation and to other posts, and in his absence, the command was variously assumed by Maj. M.M. Payne, Capt. Derrick, Maj. Dulaney, Col. Lindsay. When Gen. Wool left for good in July 1837, Lt. Col. Powell took command. Toward the end of February 1838, Lindsay decided to make New Echota the headquarters for removal.[xcviii] On May 24, 1838, Gen. Charles Renatus Floyd arrived from his home in Savannah to assume command of the Middle Military District with headquarters at New Echota. Floyd's correspondence contains one reference to a visit by Gen. Winfield Scott, in early June 1838.[xcix] A complete record of Scott's travels during the removal process could shed light on many activities that remain cloudy at this point (Illustration 13. Winfield Scott).

Illustration 13. General Winfield Scott.

Supplies. Despite of the ample time allowed to prepare for the removal of Cherokees, conditions at New Echota seemed remarkably disorganized. The post lacked axes, spades, shovels, camp and garrison equipage, nails, broadaxes, mattocks, and stationary.[c] Quartermaster Hoskins returned to Tennessee and Col. A. Cox of the Tennessee Volunteers assumed charge of the increasingly important quartermaster department. Soon after, he was given the added responsibilities of overseeing the quartermasters and stores of the posts in the counties of Murray (Ft. Hoskins and Ft. Gilmer), Walker (Ft. Cumming), and Paulding (camp at Cedar Town). In late May 1838, he was in charge of Canton (Ft. Buffington), New Echota (Ft. Wool), Spring Place (Ft. Hoskins), Paulding and Walker.[ci] As late as mid-May, one company at Ft. Wool lacked camp and garrison equipage, and the quartermaster did not have adequate mess pans, wall tents, camp kettles, and common tents.[cii] Just five days before the roundup, Cox received word that a special order for Ft. Wool had been made for hundreds of mess pans, camp kettles, and muskets, and thousands of musket cartridges and flints, as well as kegs of rifle powder, lead, and 1,600 havre sacks.[ciii] It is possible and even likely that wagons of supplies and detachments of troops and prisoners passed each other on the Federal Road leading to and from New Echota.

Companies. Just as the commanders and quartermasters at Ft. Wool changed, so too did the companies posted there. Capt. Vernon's name drops out of the Ft. Wool records. The first two Georgia companies stationed at New Echota left to establish other posts. Capt. Buffington's company went to Ft. Buffington in the fall of 1837, and about the same time Capt. Derrick's company marched to Ellijay to establish Ft. Hetzel. Capt. Tuggle's company arrived in March 1838, and was soon joined by Capt. Farriss's company from Walker County. By late May, just prior to the roundup of Cherokee prisoners, Capts. Storey, Campbell, Stell, Ellis, Bowman, Hamilton, Daniel, Horton, Brewster, and Vincent, and their companies, were encamped at New Echota. In the 48 hours prior to the roundup, a total of 18 companies left Ft. Wool.[civ] The number of men sleeping in tents, building fires, digging latrines, washing mess pans, cooking provisions, and loading guns at New Echota must have ranged from 1,000 to 2,000.

Prisoners. At each post in Georgia, the commanding officer or his subaltern was told to report the number of Indians living within a ten-mile radius. Capt. Tuggle estimated 316 Cherokees, none of whom evidenced any hostility and all of whom agreed to emigrate if Principal Chief John Ross directed them to do so.[cv] Early in the morning of May 26, 1838, Gen. Floyd led nine companies out to collect the Cherokees along the Coosawattee River approximately twelve miles from Ft. Wool. Leaving the baggage and provision wagons at Lowrey's ferry, they crossed the river and divided into small detachments that fanned out to prevent escape. By evening, they returned to their post with 209 Indians in captivity.[cvi]

Over the next week, approximately 3,000 Cherokees were captured and sent to Tennessee camps.[cvii] By June 19, Gen. Floyd could report that no Indians remained in the Middle Military District except those who were too ill to travel and they were in the possession of the troops.[cviii] Most of the Georgia militia volunteers were discharged at New Echota by July 1, 1838, and Gen. Floyd left on July 9 to return to Savannah.[cix] All that remained for the removal armies in Georgia was the sale of the public property. At New Echota, the sale occurred Aug. 13.

Many detachments of Cherokee prisoners were marched to New Echota en route to Tennessee, and virtually all commanders of posts in Georgia reported to Ft. Wool to be mustered out. Companies from Rome, Kingston, Cedar Town, Sixes, Canton, and Forsyth County all took their prisoners to Ross's Landing via headquarters at New Echota. Each post had at least one wagon and wagon master to transport baggage for the prisoners, and another wagon would have been necessary to carry the militia equipment and provisions. What is now called the Trail of Tears extended from each Cherokee home and settlement across Cherokee Georgia to the Federal Road at New Echota and on to Ross's Landing.

On March 5, 1842, the widow of Sweet Water, named Ooloocha, submitted a claim for lost property in Georgia. "The soldiers came and took us from home," she claimed, "they first surrounded our house and they took the mare while we were at work in the fields and they drove us out of doors and did not permit us to take anything with us not even a second change of clothes, only the clothes we had on, and they shut the doors after they turned us out. They would not permit any of us to enter the house to get any clothing but drove us off to a fort that was built at New Echota. They kept us in the fort about three days and then marched us to Ross's Landing. And still on foot, even our little children, and they kept us about three days at Ross's Landing and sent us off on a boat to this country."[cx]

Fort Buffington (Canton, Cherokee County)

Sources that have been most useful in the search for Ft. Buffington are the papers of John E. Wool, New York State Library, Albany, and Record Group 393 (the removal of Cherokees) available on microfilm at the National Archives and Records Administration (NARA) in East Point, Georgia. The Cherokee County Courthouse records provide considerable information about the conflicts between Cherokees and whites in Canton between 1832 and the final removal of Indians in 1838. The correspondence of Georgia Gov. George R. Gilmer yielded perhaps the most singular piece of data, the date by which Ft. Buffington was picketed, but otherwise has proven disappointing, particularly given the role Ft. Buffington played in storing arms for the militia employed in Cherokee removal.

Ft. Buffington stood close to or on the Alabama Road (now GA Highway 20) in present-day Canton, Cherokee County, south of the Etowah River and west of the Alabama Road's junction with the Federal Road. By the time of the fort's construction in the fall of 1837, whites had lived in the area for at least five years and many had been there considerably longer. Since Cherokee Georgia had been surveyed and distributed by state lottery in 1832, Ft. Buffington was built on property that had been privately owned for five years. Following the lottery, however, property changed hands and titles with such haste and frequency that information is often lacking or inaccurate about who owned or purchased lots where removal

forts may have been built. Nonetheless, the property records for the Canton area in the 1830s are fuller than those for other counties in the Cherokee homeland and hope remains that additional research will provide the necessary documentation for the post's location.

Three separate properties have been suggested as the likely location of the fort. Two of them are north of the Alabama Road. One is adjacent to and behind Harmony Primitive Baptist Church on Harmony Drive, a short road (less than one mile) that runs north from the Alabama Road (Illustration 14. Harmony Primitive Baptist Church). Long-time residents grew up hearing that the fort had stood in a pasture on Harmony Drive, and that the spring feeding Big Branch (formerly Five-Mile Creek) east of and considerably lower than the pasture had provided water for the soldiers and Cherokees. Local residents also suggested a second site, the parking area and church lot, both of which border the pasture.

Illustration 14. Harmony Primitive Baptist Church.

Use of the name "Fort Buffington" in association with various properties occurred throughout the century following the establishment of the military post. The name appears on numerous maps of the mid- to late-nineteenth century, although without any precision. On a Cherokee County map dated 1864, "Fort Buffington" appears north of the Alabama Road, supporting some local stories about the post's location. The name is also associated with a school. Established in 1868, Buffington School was purportedly a log cabin school at the fort site and possibly built from fort timbers. On an 1894 map of Cherokee County found in the local library, the cartographer placed "Ft. Buffington Academy" north of and adjacent to the church. And finally, the name is associated with a church. The *Cherokee Advance* of July 1890 reported that "quite a number of our citizens went up to the Fort (Harmony) last Sunday to hear Rev. A.B. Vaughn, Jr., and Rev. J.M. Stewart preach."[cxi] Another article in the same issue also refers to "the fort (Harmony)."[cxii] Unquestionably, the articles associate Fort Buffington with the church, school, and Harmony Drive. No records have been found, however, to confirm the school's first location, its construction, or any relationship with the fort. Nor have any records emerged to place the fort at the two church sites, lacunae that neither dismiss nor confirm them as fort locations.

Additional support for the post's location north of the Alabama Road comes from information about an early Canton resident named Nehemiah Garrison. In 1848, Garrison sold ten acres of land to the three deacons of Harmony Church.[cxiii] The church then erected a building, which was subsequently replaced by the current structure. Forty years later, a *Cherokee Advance* article stated that the fort had stood on Garrison's property, which could reasonably place it at either or both of the Harmony Church sites.

The article claims that Garrison had sued the government for damages to his property caused by the establishment and use of the fort on his land. It states that the 1860 court of claims awarded Garrison a judgment of seven hundred dollars, but the claim was forgotten because of the impending Civil War. After Garrison's death, his son John followed up on the claim and "it was not until last week," according to the article, "that he received notice from col. candler [sic] that the judgment was a matter of record and the money was ready to be paid over upon the proper showing."[cxiv]

Unfortunately, no such claim has been found in two visits to the National Archives in Washington, nor has any archivist at the Archives been able to locate the claim. Furthermore, Cherokee County historian John Carver researched the Garrison property records and found no record of Nehemiah Garrison's purchasing the land north of the Alabama Road. Moreover, Carver has pointed out that Garrison's obituary says he moved to Cherokee County in 1839, well after the property was used for the construction of a military post.[cxv] More research may determine whether Garrison owned Cherokee County property before moving there.

By 1860, "Ft. Buffington" was listed as a Cherokee County post office, indicating the presence of a small community by that name. The community persisted until the end of the century and Nehemiah Garrison's 1884 obituary states that he died at his home near Ft. Buffington. We can hope that further research will identify the entity to which the phrase "Ft. Buffington" refers, whether school, church, community, or memory.

In addition to the (absence of) evidence that calls into question the Garrison story, two site visits, one with State Archaeologist Dave Crass, all but eliminated the Harmony Church property and the lot behind it as likely places for the fort's construction. After examining the uneven terrain, one-mile distance to the Alabama Road, and the substantial elevation drop to the spring, Dave Crass and I agreed that the two church sites are unlikely.

The third site suggested by residents is on the south side of the Alabama Road in a field that stands between two streams (Illustration 15. Possible location of Fort Buffington). Joey Charles of the Office of the State Archaeologist and I visited the site and found it to have high archaeological potential (see site report). Soil auguring indicates the field is conducive to archaeology.

Illustration 15. Possible location of Fort Buffington.

Military Occupation. The military occupation of Ft. Buffington lasted from October 1837 to July 1838. Ezekial Buffington raised a company of mounted volunteers in Gainesville in the winter of 1836 and they were quickly posted to New Echota.[cxvi] In October 1837, Buffington's company moved to Canton where they erected the post. Pvt. John H. Wood was appointed quartermaster and remained in that position until removal was completed. No other company joined Buffington's. On May 11, 1838, however, an order issued from Ft. Cass for the disposition of militia in Georgia directs "the Maj. to take command at Ft. Buffington near Canton; 1 company to proceed to Ft. Buffington."[cxvii] Although the major's name is not included, later correspondence between Gen. Floyd, General Scott, and civil authorities in Canton indicate that it was Maj. Robert Pope, who offended local officials in the course of Indian removal.

Apparently Pope captured an Indian who was being sued in the Cherokee County courts. Someone complained to Scott, who turned the matter over to Floyd. While agreeing to investigate, Floyd wrote to the justices that federal treaties took precedence over state matters and that he would not permit Indians "on every little cause of litigation to be taken out of my possession."[cxviii] Pope was exonerated and the Indian remained a federal rather than a county prisoner. In a second instance, a soldier, presumably in Buffington's company, was charged with a criminal offence and "rescued himself from the custody of civil authorities." Pope apparently arrested the authorities for interfering with government operations, and Floyd ordered their release.[cxix] Although no other posts left records of altercations with local officials, conflicts over authority, behavior, and property surely arose.

The records are incomplete but it appears that Capt. Buffington turned over ordnance supplies on July 5, 1838 and Ft. Buffington was then abandoned.[cxx] The following fall, Pvt. Thomas Harney of Buffington's company faced a court martial on charges of deserting the company on June 18, and was convicted.[cxxi] No other records have yet been located that refer to the military occupation at Ft. Buffington.

Construction. While stationed at New Echota, Buffington was instructed to build winter quarters for his company according to the plan adopted by Capt. Derrick. Buffington may have used the same plan again for barracks at Ft. Buffington. Locating the plan either in the records or archaeologically will be particularly useful for both forts and generally for others. Unfortunately, the National Archives records contain numerous references to plans and maps that do not accompany the correspondence, presumably because they were removed for use. The effort to locate such important material will continue.

In the fall of 1837, Buffington's company was ordered to the neighborhood of Canton, with instructions to build huts, stables, and any other buildings necessary.[cxxii] Assuming every man in the company owned a horse, the stables would have housed more than 60 animals over a period of nine months. In addition, Buffington provided his own ox team to aid in construction, and provided his own wagons and teams for transportation. Apparently a man of means, he also proposed supplying his own corn and fodder for six months. Buffington specified costs for his supplies in a letter to Lt. A.R. Hetzel in the Quartermaster's Department at Ft. Cass.[cxxiii]

On the first of March 1838, Georgia Governor Gilmer reported that Buffington was fortified, making it the first stockaded fort beyond New Echota.[cxxiv] Construction of barracks, stables, store houses, wagon sheds, a stockade, and possibly hospital quarters made proximity to a major thoroughfare, such as the Alabama Road, important if not essential. In addition, the amount of construction and length of occupation may have left traces that can be found archaeologically.

Supplies. Lt. A.R. Hetzel at Ft. Cass was responsible for supplying the stations in the Cherokee Nation. He sent 60 barrels of flour to Ft. Buffington in the first two months of its occupancy, which implies the existence of ovens at the fort.[cxxv] Subsequently, ordnance, subsistence, medical supplies, and bundle bedding were transported by wagons that likely traveled down the Federal Road and across the Alabama Road to the fort. Records do not indicate that Buffington's company required any camp and garrison equipage other than what they received at New Echota in 1836.

As the first fortified post outside of New Echota and perhaps because it was located close to a white settlement, Ft. Buffington became one of two repositories for munitions to be distributed to other posts. Officers from other stations personally received their arms from Capt. Buffington and left statements to that effect. An average company received 60 muskets, 60 cartridge boxes, 60 cartridge belts, 60 bayonet scabbards, 60 bayonet belts, 150 flints, 1 box of cartridges, 3 kegs of powder, 300 pounds of balls, and cartridge paper.[cxxvi] Ordnance storehouses at Ft. Buffington must have been larger than those at other posts.

Prisoners. Two days after the roundup began, Buffington's company (under Maj. Pope) had captured 400 prisoners and by June 9, Gen. Floyd reported that 479 prisoners were escorted by Capt. Cox from Ft. Buffington, via headquarters, to Ross's Landing.[cxxvii] A week earlier, Floyd had expressed his frustration over the irregular pace of returns and sent his staff Brigade Major to arrest the commanders at Ft. Buffington and Sixes for not forwarding their prisoners.[cxxviii] No such arrests are recorded.

Sixes (Cherokee County)

The resource that has been most useful regarding the military encampment at the Cherokee town of Sixes has been the Ga. Dept. of Archives and History. As part of a WPA project, much of the correspondence of Gov. George Gilmer relating to the removal of Indians was typed and compiled in three bound volumes collectively identified as *Cherokee Letters, Talks, Treaties*. Housed at the Archives, the volumes contain virtually all the information I have found on the encampment. In addition, the original manuscript correspondence of the governor contains relevant information. The National Archives branch in East Point, Ga. owns microfilmed copies of the National Archives' original documents relating to Cherokee removal, and those films include information on Sixes as well as many other posts in Georgia.

During the process of research, I was contacted by a member of the Cherokee Nation, who's husband descends from the last known chief at Sixes (Chief Stop). She informed me that Stop's family carried the Sixes fire to Indian Territory and placed it at the Stomp Grounds that have been in continuous use ever since. We have stayed in contact and hope to collaborate on further research on the town as well as the encampment. She had no information on Sixes and was happy to receive the research notes I sent.

Sixes Town. Located in the Hickory Log District of the Cherokee Nation, the town of Sixes appears on numerous nineteenth century maps on the north and south sides of the Etowah River near its junction with the Little River.[cxxix] Presently, the town site lies under the waters of Lake Allatoona, a 12,000-acre recreational lake created in 1950 by a dam on the Etowah. In1987, Southeastern Archaeological Services of Athens, Georgia completed a cultural resources survey of Allatoona Lake for the U.S. Army Corps of Engineers that successfully correlated archaeological sites with records of Indian improvements in the town of Sixes.[cxxx] In other words, Sixes was geographically located even though it is inundated.

Settled about 1799, Sixes stood on the north and south banks of the Etowah River east of the Little River in the Piedmont uplands and in the Hickory Log District of the Cherokee Nation. On maps of the mid-nineteenth century, it appears to be on the south side, but in an 1834 letter to the governor, one John Brewster claimed to be living "in the heart of one of the most populous Indian settlements (The Sixes Town) on the N.W. side of the Etowah River."[cxxxi] Brewster may have moved to the area in order to mine gold.

The discovery of gold in north Georgia intensified the pressure for the removal of the Cherokees. As many as ten thousand gold-seekers poured into Georgia following the late 1829 publication of the news of gold discoveries.[cxxxii] Georgia extended its laws over the Cherokee Nation and Gov. George Gilmer was authorized to take control of Cherokee lands. Rapid developments pitted the state against the federal government as Cherokee agent Hugh Montgomery issued a prohibition against intruders on Cherokee land and the federal government sent troops to guard the mines.

A detachment under the command of Lt. Abram C. Fowler was stationed at Camp Hinar at Sixes, site of one of the richest mines in Georgia. Confusion exists to this day about Camp Hinar, which is often named as a removal post and/or called Fort Hinar, Fort Sixes, or Fort Hinar Sixes. There is a possibility that the 1838 companies occupied buildings erected by the 1830 troops, but otherwise the association of Hinar with the removal of Cherokees is wholly incorrect. In September 1830, the troops destroyed 19 buildings at Sixes in an effort to stop intruders from mining.[cxxxiii] The buildings must have housed miners or their equipment and may not have been part of the Cherokee community at all. Two months later, the federal troops were withdrawn, and in 1831, the Georgia Guard took over "the protection" of the mines for approximately one year. In May 1834, John Brewster informed the governor that the Sixes mine was closed.[cxxxiv]

In 1833, as many as 400 Cherokees lived in Sixes Town.[cxxxv] According to the 1835 census, a minimum of 26 families lived there. The census and, later, the valuations, recorded the waterways on which the Cherokees lived rather than town affiliations, and so the number of Sixes residents may have been considerably larger. Cherokee County courthouse records of 1835 mention a town house at Sixes.[cxxxvi] One Sixes resident was the relatively affluent Moses Downing, who owned a ferry where the Alabama Road crossed the Etowah River.[cxxxvii] All residents opposed the treaty and some refused to talk to the census takers or evaluators. In 1842, many former residents of Sixes submitted claims for compensation lost in Georgia. Chief Stop signed as a witness for several claims, which bring life to the otherwise nameless individuals rounded up by the militia in 1838.

Military Occupation. More militia companies were stationed at Sixes than at any other post in Georgia, which supports the possibility that the town remained populous. On May 11, 1838 an order was sent from Ft. Cass for a colonel, major, and seven companies to take post at Sixes, but subsequent invoices indicate that the actual number at the post was five.[cxxxviii] The militia companies of Capts. John D. Stell of Fayette County (79 men), James T. Ellis of Henry County (64 men), Thomas H. Bowman of Elbert County (70 men), Mathew T. Hamilton of Gwinnett County (38 men), and James Daniel of Madison County (73 men) totaled 324 soldiers.[cxxxix]

The most detailed description of the removal process comes from one of the soldiers stationed at Sixes. On June 6, 1838, N. W. Pittman of Daniel's Madison Company wrote to his father-in-law, wife, children, "and all inquiring friends." He said the company left in the evening of May 28 and traveled until midnight taking prisoners, then camped. "Some of us lay in the Road, some in a house with the Red people, the balance in another house which we had taken an Indian and his wife and placed them all together. Some occupied the Indian bed before it was cold and some under the same. The balance stretched on the floor until there was no room for any more." When morning came, they left the prisoners with a guard and continued from house to house taking captives and leaving guards until nearly all were posted. They returned to camp about 2 p.m. with a total of 92 captives, and met the other companies who had returned. The total number of prisoners taken in the 24-hour period was 927.[cxl]

On June 9, 1838, Gen. Floyd ordered three of the five companies to leave Sixes. Capt. Stell's company was one of two that escorted a detachment of prisoners to Ross's Landing, but records do not show which other companies were still at the encampment.[cxli]

Construction. No information has been found about the construction that may have occurred at Sixes. Although the companies apparently camped rather than build a stockade, they may have stabled their several hundred horses, constructed ovens for cooking, or maintained a blacksmith shop. Lacking the opportunity for further archaeological investigation, we remain hopeful that additional primary records will be found to fill in the story.

Supplies. While stationed at New Echota, the companies received muskets, cartridge boxes, cartridge box belts, bayonet belts, bayonet scabbards, belt plats, picks, wipers, spring vices, musket ball cartridges, musket flints, gun slings, and team drivers.[cxlii] On May 26, 1838, invoices were sent for 12 teams that had gone to Sixes, possibly to carry infirm and elderly prisoners or Cherokee possessions.[cxliii] Plans were made in mid-June for the sale of all public property left at several of the posts, including Sixes.[cxliv] In the fall, Capt. John H. King, commander of the Cherokee (County?) Volunteers stationed at the Sixes, informed Gov. Gilmer that he had notified his company to return all public arms and accoutrements.[cxlv] King apparently was not a part of the removal companies stationed at Sixes but instead, presumably, was part of a Cherokee County company whose weapons were stored in the court house.

Prisoners. On June 2, 1838, Gen. Floyd wrote that the officers at Sixes had not yet sent their prisoners. He had sent his staff Brigade Major to Sixes to order the Indians on to Ross's Landing and to arrest the malingering commander if necessary.[cxlvi] Four days later, 825 Indians arrived at Ft. Wool from Sixes. They were escorted by two companies and were on their way to Ross's Landing.[cxlvii] The total number removed from Sixes by June 9, 1838 was 950.[cxlviii]

Fort Floyd (Dahlonega, Lumpkin County)

The most helpful sources for Ft. Floyd, Dahlonega, are the National Archives records of the Quartermaster's Department. Initially, we were not certain that any kind of post was established in Dahlonega, but the commitment of Trail of Tears charter members Dan and Dola Davis encouraged considerable research. The 1954 location of a state historical marker at a site called "The Station" five miles south of Dahlonega complicated the process since no primary documents could be found to connect the Station to the removal of Indians. The 1932 publication of Andrew W. Cain's *History of Lumpkin County* convinced many readers that

"The Station" was the site of Gen. Scott's headquarters where "hundreds of Indians were brought."[cxlix] Cain's source was a published (but not referenced) article by Col. W. P. Price, whose father was said to have participated in the removal. Other writers followed Cain and used various names for the post at Dahlonega including Ft. Dahlonega and Ft. Lumpkin, neither of which existed.

Correspondence found in the Georgia Department of Archives and History refers to Camp Dahlonega and Cantonment Dahlonega, indicating the 1838 existence of an unfortified post. In contrast to the information on the historical marker, no evidence has emerged to connect the 1830 occupation of gold mine areas with the site of the removal post. Two trips to the National Archives in Washington uncovered a trove of material relating to Ft. Floyd and its role in the distribution of subsistence supplies to four other posts. We are now certain that the militia constructed a fort in Dahlonega in conjunction with the removal of Indians. It is unlikely that any Cherokee prisoners were ever kept in a camp or garrison in Dahlonega, but since the records from Gen. Eustis in North Carolina have not been located (and the garrison in Dahlonega reported to Ft. Butler), we cannot yet be certain.

Dahlonega. Dahlonega, from the Cherokee word *taloni ge* (yellow), was incorporated at the December, 1833 session of the state legislature. Previously called Licklog, the town was made the seat of Lumpkin County, which was created in 1832 and named for Gov. Wilson Lumpkin. Gold had been found in the nearby Chestatee River as early as 1828, which led to a population explosion of itinerants as well as settlers. By the time of its incorporation, Dahlonega already had a log courthouse, soon followed by dozens of houses, stores, taverns, and more than a thousand residents.[cl] In 1836, the log courthouse was replaced by one of brick and mortar.[cli]

The importance of Dahlonega in the larger economy is evidenced by construction of the Dahlonega branch of the U.S. Mint, which began in 1835. Located on a ten-acres tract on a knoll south of the town square, the site chosen for the mint already had a working well and several buildings.[clii] Between 1835 and the commencement of removal in May 1838, workmen struggled with fifty thousand pounds of mint machinery and construction materials. The first coins were minted April 17, 1838, scarcely a month before removal began.[cliii] The presence of the mint and the abundance of gold were important factors in the decision to establish a post in town. As it turned out, the presence of the mint affected the selection of the site for the post.

Since Dahlonega was incorporated by the state legislature, it was never considered a Cherokee town. Its location in the foothills of the Blue Ridge with proximity to the Chestatee and Etowah Rivers and Cane and Yahoola Creeks made it a desirable location for white settlement. Nearby lay the established Cherokee communities of Frog Town, Chestatee Old Town, Bread Town, Amicalola, Tensawattee Town, and Big Savannah. Many Cherokees along the Chestatee and its tributaries signed up for emigration in 1832, but as late as 1836, at least 17 Cherokee families lived on Tennsawattee Creek, 28 on Amicalola Creek, and more than 13 in Big Savannah on the Etowah River.[cliv] Along the Etowah just west of Dahlonega, whites who had intermarried with Cherokees farmed sizeable plantations. Daniel Davis, Silas Palmour, and three Davis sons-- William, Martin, and John—owned homes, orchards, mills, slaves, and river land as well as upland.[clv] All were considered citizens of the Cherokee Nation.

Military Occupation. Records reveal an unusual amount of confusion regarding the militia occupation of Dahlonega. Apparently the lines of authority were not established since Gilmer, Scott, and various members of the quartermaster's department were all making military decisions. In December of 1837, Gilmer called for an infantry company to be stationed in Dahlonega but did not specify which one.[clvi] At the end of January, Gilmer wrote that Capt. Lewis Long's Habersham Rifles were going to Dahlonega but Long then disappears from the records.[clvii] In early February, Gilmer again wrote that a recently-received (unnamed) Georgia company would be posted to Dahlonega, but soon afterwards Gen. Scott sent a Tennessee company commanded by Capt. Peake to the site.[clviii]

Meanwhile, local residents competed with one another to enter the service, and Gilmer received numerous letters of protest from frustrated citizens who considered themselves the most valid members of the Dahlonega volunteers. Finally, in mid-February, two months after Gilmer's first call, Capt. Peake arrived in Dahlonega with quartermaster A.M. Julian, who selected a position "as near the U.S. Mint as I could."[clix] On Feb. 26, however, the Mint supervisor wrote Gilmer that "the company destined for this place" had not arrived and he had heard that they were not coming.[clx]

The final occupation was not yet set. Georgia militia Cpt. (Lewis) Levy of Habersham County and (1st Lt. James?) McGinnis (of Gwinnet County) were reported ready for muster and posting to Dahlonega on the first of March.[clxi] Less than two weeks later, Capt. Peake's quartermaster wrote that he had learned that Levy could not raise his company and would, therefore, not come to Dahlonega.[clxii] Peake's company left soon after and in mid-March, Capt. Benjamin Cleveland, Jr. of Franklin County was assigned to take command of the post.[clxiii] Although he arrived unsure of his final command, Cleveland remained until the completion of removal.

Cleveland was a seasoned soldier, having served in the War of 1812 under Andrew Jackson. When he mustered in at Ft. Butler, North Carolina for the removal of Cherokees, he was 46 years old and commanded a company of 93 men.[clxiv] Important details regarding Cleveland's command remain unknown because he was assigned to the Eastern Military District under the command of Gen. Eustis, whose records were not found in the National Archives. Additional research will be necessary to find more about Cleveland in this unusually important post.

In addition to Julian, Lt. A. Montgomery acted as Dahlonega quartermaster for some part of March. Pvt. James Ratcliff served as Cleveland's quartermaster, but by April 8, V. M. Campbell arrived from Ft. Foster to supervise the quartermaster departments at Dahlonega, Coosawattee (Ft. Gilmer), Ellijay (Ft. Hetzel), and Sanders (Ft. Newnan). Campbell later received responsibility for the camp at Chastain's as well. Ratcliff remained, however, even though he pointed out to Lt. Hetzel of the quartermaster department at Ft. Cass that he had no experience.[clxv]

The correspondence between Campbell and Lt. A.R. Hetzel provides substantial detail about the provisions distributed and the visits made to various posts throughout the removal period. The data indicate that companies maintained relatively good contact with one another even though sites in the Cherokee Nation were often described as remote, unknown, and set in a wilderness. The data also suggest that the purchase of corn and fodder, the hiring of transport wagons, and the leasing of local rooms for offices and housing surely enriched numerous merchants.

Construction. Although no specific evidence has been found regarding construction at the Dahlonega post, certain aspects can be inferred. The post at Dahlonega was referred to as a camp or cantonment until May 8, 1838, after which time it was called a fort. Col. Lindsay had determined on March 1 that all posts "hereafter occupied" would be defended by stockades, and April 16 Cleveland received specific orders to erect barracks for his men.[clxvi] We can assume, therefore, that the fort consisted minimally of a picket and barracks. In addition, Cleveland's company was mounted, which suggests the construction of stables or some kind of paddock for the horses, and storage facilities for the corn and fodder to feed them. The post included a medical department that could have consisted of a tent or a hut. Additionally, Cleveland was given permission for a blacksmith and tools for the upkeep of equipment, which could have resulted in a smithy's shed.[clxvii] Quartermaster Campbell was responsible for the wagon teams to supply the five posts in his division and their supply of forage as well. Whether buildings were furnished for the horses and/or wagons has not yet been determined. There were undoubtedly some buildings in town that Cleveland could utilize for some of the fort's needs, but no invoice for such expenses has appeared in the quartermasters records. Moreover, there was at one time a site in Dahlonega known as the Old Barracks, considered a militia mustering ground.[clxviii] Its possible connection with Ft. Floyd has not been determined.

Supplies. Ft. Floyd, along with forts Wool and Buffington, became a repository for arms and supplies that were distributed to other posts. As early as March 4, Lt. Hetzel was requesting invoices for the camp and government equipage, subsistence, and ordnance sent to Dahlonega. After Cleveland arrived, he took part of the new brick courthouse for the ordnance and ordnance stores, which were considerable. On April 14, more than 7,000 pounds of arms arrived from Augusta as well as an 82 pound box of flints.[clxix] References to subsistence and/or camp and garrison equipage sent from Ft. Cass to

Dahlonega occurred on March 19, March 24 (when the bacon rations were short), April 3, and May 8.[clxx]

Prisoners. The lack of records from Ft. Butler proved most frustrating on the question of the number of prisoners taken by the Ft. Floyd company. Prior to Eustis's arrival at Ft. Butler, Cleveland wrote to Gen. Scott that he planned to lead 60 men to the Tensawattee or Big Savannah Town the following day for the purpose of capturing Cherokees, but no further report was found in the records.[clxxi] Since the Ft. Wool records found to this point do not refer to the arrival or sending of prisoners from Ft. Floyd, we can assume that Cleveland began reporting to Eustis soon after he wrote Gen. Scott.

Fort Hetzel (Ellijay, Gilmer County)

Information on Ft. Hetzel has come primarily from the National Archives reports of the Quartermaster's Department and the microfilm rolls of Cherokee removal located at the archives branch in East Point, Georgia. Local Trail of Tears member Leslie Thomas has investigated numerous leads. In addition, two county histories by Lawrence L. Stanley have been published and are considered valuable by local contacts: *The Gilmer County Area of Georgia 200 Years ago and Pages from Gilmer County History 1832-1977* and *A Little History of Gilmer County.* George Gordon Ward's *Annals of Upper Georgia Centered in Gilmer County* includes the names of many early white settlers and local landmarks, and a sketch of Ft. Hetzel based on "careful research by the Author and artist, Robert C. Adams." Ward claims "the severely simple fort stood until about 1868."[clxxii] The books by Stanley and Ward both contain

excerpts from the 1835-38 day book kept by store owner Coke A. Ellington.

Sometime prior to 1984, Lawrence Stanley placed a stone and granite boulder marking the place he believed to be the site of Ft. Hetzel, at the intersection of Yukon Road and Highway 515, now occupied by Wal-Mart (Illustration 16. Fort Hetzel marker). When grading for road construction was about to destroy the site, Stanley moved the boulder about a mile away to the intersection of 1st Street and Highway 515, where it now stands. A local resident recalls that the Georgia Department of Transportation managed the road construction, but contacts at DOT have no record of recovering archaeological materials from the site. Stanley and Ward are both deceased and efforts to discover their sources have been unsuccessful.

Illustration 16. Fort Hetzel marker.

Ellijay. The town of Ellijay in the Appalachian province was made the county seat of Gilmer in 1834, just two years after the county was created. By the time of removal, it had a courthouse, stores, a post office, and residences. Ellijay was a Cherokee settlement known as *elatse yi* (fresh green vegetation), or some variant, at least since the eighteenth century, and in the early nineteenth century was included in the Cherokee Nation district of Coosawattee. The white settlement developed on the west bank of the Ellijay River at its junction with the Cartecay. Since the joined streams become the Coosawattee River, Ellijay stood at the head of an important waterway where many Cherokees lived. Whites began moving into the area in greater numbers as soon as the county was created and gold was discovered. As indicated by the accounts in the Coke Ellington Day Book, whites and Cherokees lived, or at least shopped, virtually side-by-side until the commencement of removal. White Path, one of the most prominent leaders in Cherokee history, lived just north of Ellijay and died on the Trail of Tears in Hopkinsville, Kentucky.

Other Cherokee settlements in the area included Board Town on the upper Ellijay, Mountain Town, Turnip Town (now White Path), Cartecay, and Cherry Log. According to the 1836 evaluations, 20 Cherokee families owned improvements in Mountain Town, 10 at Turnip Town (including White Path), and five on the Ellijay River.[clxxiii] Many improvements were never evaluated, as is mentioned frequently in the Cherokee claims submitted from the Indian Territory, so we can be confident that many more Cherokees lived in and were removed from the area.

Military Occupation. The military occupation of the Ellijay post began in the fall of 1837. Capt. William Derrick, who had been called into service in 1836 and stationed at New Echota since then, was ordered to proceed "to the neighborhood of Jones's" near Ellijay to select a suitable position for the post. Derrick was accompanied by his mounted company including Pvt. James J. Field, quartermaster.[clxxiv] Further research may identify Jones, who has remained elusive in county courthouse records to this point. On Oct. 7, 1837, Derrick was positioned near the mouth of the Ellijay

River.[clxxv] As with other posts from Dahlonega east to the North Carolina border, Derrick was assigned to the Eastern Military District under the command of Gen. Abram Eustis.

At Derrick's request, Ft. Wool quartermaster Cox selected the site for his post, which Cox named in honor of supervising quartermaster Lt. A.R. Hetzel. Cox acknowledged that the site, located on the Cartecay River about one mile east of the courthouse, was "objectionable in the military point" but had good access to wood, water, and forage.[clxxvi] If Cox's assessment of the distance was correct, the post stood somewhere in East Ellijay. In mid-March, 1838, Capt. Donaldson's infantry company joined Derrick's mounted company at Ft. Hetzel, bringing the number of militia to well over one hundred.[clxxvii]

At least one local resident agreed with Cox's assessment of the objectionable site. William Cole wrote the governor on March 1 that the troops were stationed at a most inconvenient location where they could protect neither the town nor the countryside. With evident dismay Cole's reported that the commanders failed to send scouts to watch Indian "maneuvering" and actually told the Indians they had come to protect them.[clxxviii]

Following the capture and removal of Indians, Derrick was ordered to relieve Capt. John Dorsey at Ft. Newnan, and to arrest him if necessary.[clxxix] Such orders indicate the extent to which Derrick had earned the respect of his commanding officers. Although Derrick's was one of only two companies still in service on July 9, he apparently had been mustered out by July 19, 1838.[clxxx]

Construction. Following the assignment of commands, Derrick's first orders were to erect huts and stables for the company and other buildings as necessary, "according to the plan herewith furnished." The same orders were issued at the same time to Capt.

Ezekial Buffington, and, as in other cases, no plan remains in the collection of military correspondence.[clxxxi]No other comments about construction at Ft. Hetzel have been found to this point, but we can assume Derrick built storage facilities for subsistence, forage, and munitions. In late March, quartermaster Field reported that he had cut a road from Coosawattee (Ft. Gilmer and the Federal Road) to Ft. Hetzel, thereby diminishing the travel and transport time from southern points.[clxxxii]

Supplies. Ft. Hetzel began receiving supplies from Ft. Cass in December 1837. The sending of 36 barrels of flour in one December week indicates that storage facilities and cooking areas, possibly with ovens, were complete by that time.[clxxxiii] More flour was sent in January 1838. By the end of the month, an order had been placed for 30,000 rations, 7,500 bushels of corn, and a proportionate amount of hay or fodder.[clxxxiv] In early March more subsistence was ordered from Ft. Cass and by April the quartermaster at Ft. Hetzel was in debt.[clxxxv]

From one of Derrick's queries to Lt. Hetzel, we learn of a removal policy that has heretofore remained unknown. On June 1, Derrick wrote for instructions on foraging the ponies of the prisoners since grass was scarce and there was none near the fort. "I have been instructed by the major general," he wrote, "to use them as pack horses."[clxxxvi]

Prisoners. An altercation at Ft. Hetzel remains one of the few documented in the records. A member of Derrick's company knocked down an Indian woman who had "struck at him with a stick and tried to get his gun." Derrick reproved the man but gave no

word about the condition of the woman.[clxxxvii] The incident was reported to Gen. Eustis, who expressed satisfaction with Derrick's explanation.[clxxxviii]

Derrick's capture of Indians was swift and efficient. By May 28, two days after the roundup commenced, he held 425-450 captives and did not think he could handle more because "they run in every instance." He attributed his success to the fact that he had not taken time to collect Indian possessions and that he had broken up families so that runaways would come in more willingly.[clxxxix] On June 4, Derrick was still waiting for wagons to arrive and help with the transport of captives. He felt ready to send 500, and was pleased that he had captured head men such as Young Buck, Old Hemp, and Kingfisher. He also reported that someone had mistakenly brought in White Path's family but he had released them.[cxc] In late June, Derrick sent in an additional 84 Indians for a total of 884 captives, one of the highest totals from the Georgia posts.[cxci]

Fort Gilmer (Rock Springs, Murray County)

Useful data about Ft. Gilmer has come from both the National Archives (especially the quartermaster's records) and its branch at East Point, the National Archives Records Administration (the microfilm reels of the papers relating to the removal of Cherokees). Murray County Courthouse records are unusually complete regarding deeds and land transfers, and further research in those records may yield useful references. The land on which Ft. Gilmer is thought to have stood has remained intact and in the same family since the removal era. The Hemphill/Swanson family has been cooperative and interested in identifying the post's exact location. Retired state employee Phil Hackney (a parks ranger with DNR) has lived and worked in the area many years and is well informed about pot hunting at the site.

Other local sources also were helpful. In 1988, Tim R. Howard led the Murray County History Committee to produce *Murray County Heritage,* a history that contains considerable material about early county conflicts between whites and Indians and a useful chronology of military developments in the county. While lacking new information about the post, the book will be of particular use in subsequent work that details the period when Indians were expelled from Georgia. The proximity of the Vann House and the Moravian mission at Spring Place resulted in abundant records about everything from weather to farming conditions in the vicinity where the post was later built (Illustration 17. The Van House).

Illustration 17. The Vann House.

Sometime in the 1950s, the Georgia Historical Commission erected a state marker near the likely site of Ft. Gilmer (Illustration 18. Fort Gilmer Historical Marker). The marker contains several egregious errors, including identification of the date of the New Echota Treaty as 1833 rather than 1835, the statement that there were "seven such forts" in the "Cherokee territory," and the claim that Ft. Gilmer was the temporary headquarters of Winfield Scott. Replacing the marker with accurate Trail of Tears signage is imperative.

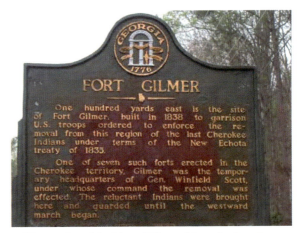

Illustration 18. Fort Gilmer historical maker.

The site has been a target of pothunters for some time. Phil Hackney, who once encountered two Tennessee men leaving the site with metal detectors, said the site was well known and often visited by pothunters. One of the property owners once found a military buckle that dated to the removal period in a shop in a neighboring town. The shop owner said the buckle had come from Ft. Gilmer.

Ft. Gilmer stood on the Federal Road near the Cherokee town of Coosawattee, one of the largest, most populous, and longest-occupied towns in the Cherokee Nation, attributes that doubtless led to the post's establishment. The settlement first came to the attention of Europeans in the sixteenth century when Spanish conquistadores identified the chiefdom of Coosa, then occupied by Muskhogean speakers. In the following two centuries the site became the Cherokee town of Coosawattee.

The town doubtless derived its name from the Coosawattee River, along which it extended on both sides for as much as five miles. Its southern terminus was the junction of the Coosawattee and Talking Rock Creek. The importance of the river, and perhaps the town as well, to the Cherokee Nation is evident from the fact that Coosawattee was also the name of one of the eight Cherokee Districts. The Federal Road ran the length of the town and, when it was first constructed in the early 1800s, some enterprising residents built a toll-gate across the thoroughfare.

In 1823, the Baptists opened a mission and school at Coosawattee, under the direction of London-born Thomas Dawson and his wife. When the mission became a preaching station as well, the Coosawattee residents often gathered for services at the home of one of the Cherokee Nation's wealthiest and most influential members, Judge John Martin. Martin also sent one of his children to the Baptist mission school.[cxcii] The Baptist missionary from the Valley Towns, Evan Jones, visited Coosawattee on numerous occasions and usually stayed at Martin's home.[cxciii] When Dawson was persuaded to leave Coosawattee for the Valley Town mission the following year, Martin offered to pay the ABCFM for another teacher. In spite of the Baptist initiatives, however, missionary Butrick referred to Coosawattee as "that dark place," a reliable indication of the community's continuing cultural conservatism.[cxciv]

Coosawattee remained on the Baptist preaching circuit even after the school and mission closed (five months after its opening), and in the summer of 1836, Evan Jones found a great increase of interest in conversion. More than 20 Cherokees were baptized, some in Talking Rock Creek, in 1836-37. In 1838, the pace accelerated. Convert and missionary Jesse Bushyhead baptized 47 fellow Cherokees in May, 10 days before removal began.[cxcv]

While Martin, with 69 slaves and 315 acres of improved land, was unquestionably the wealthiest Cherokee at Coosawattee, his neighbor John Adair Bell was also affluent and influential. A member of the Treaty Party and

signer of the treaty, Bell owned a two-story house, store house, smoke house, shuck house, corn cribs, stables, a dairy, slaves, and more than 100 acres of improved land.[cxcvi] In 1836, Bell became the disbursing or issuing agent for "poor and destitute Cherokees" in Coosawattee. He traveled to Calhoun, Tennessee to pick up rations made available by the federal government and was ordered to use the distribution as an opportunity to impress upon the recipients the necessity of complying with the treaty. Agent Albert Lenoir at New Echota told him which Cherokees were allowed to receive rations.[cxcvii]

An estimated 600 Cherokees lived at Coosawattee at the time of removal.[cxcviii] Moreover, hundreds of Creeks had taken refuge in or near Coosawattee and a few other Cherokee settlements after they were forced from their homes in Georgia. One of the military's earliest initiatives at Coosawattee was the capture of refugee Creeks living there.

In 1977, construction was completed on Carter's Dam, the highest earth-filled dam east of the Mississippi.[cxcix] Impounding the waters of the Coosawattee River, the dam created Carter's Lake, which flooded the site of Coosawattee Town.

Military Occupation. The military occupation of Coosawattee began in late March 1837, when Capt. William Derrick was ordered there from New Echota to capture runaway and refugee Creeks. One of John Bell's female slaves served as interpreter for Derrick, who was instructed to treat the Creeks humanely if they surrendered willingly.[cc] Subsequently, Derrick was order to tell the Coosawattee Cherokees that any who helped the Creeks escape or otherwise avoid capture would be "taken forthwith and emigrated to Arkansas."[cci] Bell and Walter Sanders (also spelled Saunders) were expected to be of assistance to Derrick in his endeavors.

In mid-March, Capt. Charles W. Bond of Franklin County and his mounted company of 67 men prepared to leave New Echota for Coosawattee., and by March 31 were in place.[ccii] The company quartermaster was W. S. Howard, a businessman variously described as worthy, intelligent, and new.[cciii] Although no orders have been found regarding the assignment of additional troops to Ft. Gilmer, a May 24 list of the distribution of companies indicates that Capts. Horton and Brewster were there.[cciv] John Horton of Jackson County was activated on May 4, and Sherif Brewster of Walton County on May 7.[ccv] In late May, Maj. Blueford Venable reported the number of prisoners taken, and the same day Capt. Crane and two companies were ordered to Ft. Gilmer to take charge of the prisoners.[ccvi] Crane likely was part of a Tennessee company since his name is not found in the records of Georgia volunteers, nor is that of his commander, Lt. Col. J. B. Crane. Bond's company mustered out from New Echota on July 1.[ccvii]

In early June, Floyd wrote to Gen. Scott about an act of violence that had occurred in the vicinity of Ft. Gilmer. Floyd had received word from the post that a bailiff who had beaten and "half-hanged an Indian" near the post had been arrested, presumably by the post authorities, and was in custody.[ccviii] No other records mention the incident but further research on the subject is important if the final accounting of Cherokee trauma and loss is to be documented.

Construction. When Bond's company was order to Coosawattee in late March, they were sent to Rock Springs, four miles west of the Coosawattee River on the Federal Road.[ccix] The site may have been where Capt. Derrick encamped the previous year when he hunted for the refugee Creeks. Post construction must have proceeded during April, for as May began, quartermaster Howard requested iron suitable for the hinges for the main gate and the cross bar. Apparently he was unable to procure iron in the vicinity.[ccx] By that time, the post was named Ft. Gilmer, obviously in honor of the Georgia governor. Bond's mounted company would also have required stables for horses and storage facilities for the considerable amount of provisions sent to the post.

Supplies. Since Ft. Gilmer came under the authority of Col. Cox at New Echota, much of the useful information about the post comes from the relatively thorough quartermaster files.[ccxi] In late March, just a few days after the company arrived, Hetzel received bills of lading for the post's subsistence.[ccxii] Less than one month later, additional bills of lading were received, and the following week Howard commented on the bills for the last four loads of flour he had received as well as the 300 pounds of salt.[ccxiii] By May 1, Ft. Gilmer had on hand 5,000 bushels of corn and 850 bundles of fodder.[ccxiv] Four days later, Howard reported 6-700 bushels of corn and 8-900 bundles of fodder. By that time Howard was contracting with a vendor in Bradley County, Tennessee, because forage was running short in Murray County.[ccxv]

Howard continued to receive subsistence for the post throughout June. He and Bond disagreed on the amount of fodder to distribute to the animals, Bond insisting that it be weighed and Howard wishing to distribute it by the bundle.[ccxvi] The capture of prisoners necessitated the distribution of more rations, and, in cases where the companies allowed the prisoners to bring their livestock, forage distribution became more complex. At Ft. Gilmer, the ponies and cattle of the prisoners were sent into a ten-acre field owned by prosperous settler Farish Carter, where they completely eliminated the oats.[ccxvii] As wagons and teams arrived to transport prisoners and their possessions, the responsibilities of the quartermaster increased again. On June 3, Howard issued to the teams 12 bushels of corn, rations for four days.[ccxviii] By the end of the month, arrangements had been made for the sale of remaining public stores at the post, and Campbell arrived at Ft. Gilmer on Friday, July 6, to supervise the auction.[ccxix]

Prisoners. Two days after removal began, Maj. Venable reported that 254 prisoners were under guard at Ft. Gilmer. That same day, by separate letter, Venable stated his reluctance to send the prisoners "in their present condition" since the roundup had been so swift they had not been able to collect their possessions. The wagons had not arrived, which delayed the transport of the Cherokees.[ccxx] Three days later, Floyd wrote that Venable had escorted 109 Indians to Ross's Landing, and five days afterwards sent 225 (more?).[ccxxi] No record has been found that determines whether the "half-hanged" Indian was among them.

In the winter of 1840, new Coosawattee resident Ben Poore wrote to a friend about his thriving plantation that was five miles long and occupied an entire valley between the mountains. With 300 slaves and 3 white overseers, he was raising cattle, sugar beets, and grapes, as well as Indian corn and small grain. "The little cabins and wigwams of the Indians," he wrote, "which are scattered about among the mountains and on the water courses from which they were driven and also the graves of their friends from which they were so unwilling to be removed makes one melancholy to look at, but still it was no doubt for all the best."[ccxxii] He made no mention of the fort.

Fort Newnan (Blaine, Pickens County)

Information about Ft. Newnan was recovered at the National Archives records of the quartermaster's department and the collection of Cherokee removal records on microfilm at the National Archives Records Administration in East Point, Georgia. The records from these repositories seem relatively thin for the post, particularly in light of the discipline problems that arose soon after removal. As with other posts east of Dahlonega, Ft. Newnan was in the Eastern Military District commanded by Gen. Eustis, and when his records are located it is likely we will find additional information about all of Georgia's eastern posts.

Ft. Newnan was built in the Hickory Log District of the Cherokee Nation and stood on the south side of the Federal Road, south of Talking Rock Creek near its confluence with Town Creek. The post was likely named to honor Gen. Daniel Newnan, a Revolutionary War hero, Georgia Secretary of State (1825), and U.S. Congressman.

The Rev. Charles Walker and other local citizens are confident the post was at the junction of Highway 136 and Antioch Church Road, east of and adjacent to the present-day Blaine Masonic Lodge. Rev. Walker produced two books about Cherokee history in Pickens County. In one of them, he specifies the fort's location and states that a cemetery behind the Lodge contains the burials of Cherokees who died at the fort. He also claims that the Antioch Baptist Church was organized in one of the fort's buildings and that Fransis Mullinax [sic] purchased the church building, moved it, and rebuilt it as his home. According to Walker, in 1989 the fort-church-Mullinax home was dismantled and moved to Cherokee County, North Carolina.[ccxxiii]

Although his books do not identify his sources, Walker is locally regarded as an expert on Cherokee history. Primarily on the basis of his opinion, the

Georgia chapter of the Trail of Tears Association erected a marker at the site on March 25, 2000.

Blaine is the modern name for the former communities of Talking Rock and Sanderstown. The Cherokee settlement nearest Ft. Newnan was the community referred to as Sanderstown, which took its name from the family of Mitchell Sanders (also spelled Saunders), a white man who married a Cherokee woman, Susannah, and settled in the area. They had five sons who lived in close proximity. Their son George was the wealthy owner of several houses and slaves, stables, corncribs, smokehouses, a fish trap, and orchards, as well as a hundred acres of cleared and fenced upland. His brother John was also wealthy, with homes, slaves, 93 acres of valuable cleared land, orchards, a fish trap, a tavern, and a grist mill.[ccxxiv] The prominence and wealth of the Sanders family make sense of the repeated references to a fort to be built "near Sanders'." Both lived on the Federal Road, and Walker places the fort on the southwest portion of John Sanders' property.[ccxxv]

The connection between the Sanders family and the Carmel Mission may have influenced the location of the fort. The American Board of Commissioners for Foreign Missions established the Taloney (Talona, later Carmel) Mission and school (opened 1819) on Talking Rock Creek where the Ellijay Road joined the Federal Road. The missionaries also served as postmasters, which meant the location was familiar to Cherokees and whites, and stages had traveled to the site over the years. George Sanders lived directly across the Federal Road from the mission, and his brother John owned the lot on the southwest side of George's

property. When Carmel missionary Daniel S. Butrick left Georgia in 1835, he entrusted the mission improvements to brother Andrew Sanders, who had converted to Christianity and served as the interpreter and deacon at Carmel.[ccxxvi] The mission's fields, gardens, and buildings may have been useful to the men stationed at Ft. Newnan. The role of missionaries, particularly Butrick, as defender of the Cherokees should be noted in any signage placed at Georgia removal sites.

Cherokee communities near Ft. Newnan included Talking Rock, Talona, and Mountain Town. The 1835 census recorded at least 14 families on Seare (also spelled Scare) Corn Creek, and 24 on Talking Rock Creek. The 1836 evaluations recorded improvements of nine families on Taloney Creek and 20 families in Mountain Town.[ccxxvii] At the time of removal, the military records list 85 Cherokees living on Polecat Creek, 60 in Talona Town, 70 on Town Creek, 90 in Talking Rock, 100 on "Tearcorn" Creek, 12 on the head of "Seticoa," 200 on Hickory Log and Long Swamp Creeks, 300 on Little River, and 100 at "Tensawattee Bread Town."[ccxxviii] Doubtless, some people were removed from Ft. Hetzel by the militia; many would have been the responsibility of the company at Ft. Newnan.

Military Occupation. Ft. Newnan was established near Sanders' on the Federal Road but for a time, consideration was given to a post near Blackburn's public house, which was also located on the Federal Road. Blackburn married a Cherokee woman and opened his public house soon after the War of 1812. In 1819, President Monroe and Secretary of War John C. Calhoun stayed at Blackburn's on a tour of the South. In 1825, Blackburn opened a trade store in the same area "occupied advantagely [sic] by a Mr. Scudders."[ccxxix] Early letters propose posts at Dahlonega, Coosawattee, Ellijay, and Blackburn's.[ccxxx]

References to a "post at Sanders'" began in late March 1838 and continued until the end of April, when the post was identified as Ft. Newnan.[ccxxxi] The Rev. John Dorsey, captain, and his mounted company of 64 men were ordered to the post at the end of March.[ccxxxii] A businessman named N. J. Mays, who was not a member of the company, was appointed quartermaster.[ccxxxiii] As with other posts east of Dahlonega, Ft. Newnan was assigned to the Eastern Military District under Eustis's command, and, as with other eastern posts, data is limited at this point.

In late March, Hetzel decided to subdivide the quartermaster departments in Georgia, and he assigned Ft. Newnan to Col. Campbell at Ft. Floyd.[ccxxxiv] When the disposition of Georgia troops was made just prior to the removal of Indians, an unidentified lieutenant colonel was ordered to take command at Ft. Newnan.[ccxxxv] Although the May 17 report of the volunteer posts in the Cherokee Nation lists only one company stationed at Ft. Newnan, Eustis wrote in late June that he would order Ft. Newnan's two companies to report in to Gen. Floyd.[ccxxxvi] Since all other data indicate the post was occupied by one company, we assume that Eustis was mistaken.

Following the roundup, conditions at Ft. Newnan deteriorated. In defiance of orders, Capt. Dorsey refused to abandon the post or turn over government property. Capt. William Derrick of Ft. Hetzel, having sent someone to investigate, reported that Dorsey's company was a "complete mob," Dorsey had gone home to Hall County, and half the men were absent.[ccxxxvii] In the meantime, Dorsey wrote to Eustis "begging" to have the company retained until September, but Eustis refused. Dorsey was again ordered to leave and Derrick was ordered to arrest him if he failed to comply in a reasonable time.[ccxxxviii]

No information has surfaced to explain Dorsey's behavior or his request to continue in service, and on the morning of June 30, Maj. Payne mustered out Dorsey and his company. Dorsey's dismissal may have circumvented disciplinary action since Payne wrote that he had mustered them out before receiving the letter from Lt. Anderson at Ft. Cass.[ccxxxix] In early July, Capt. N. P. Dodson of the Tennessee Volunteers wrote from Ft. Newnan that he had arrived to convey Indian prisoners to Ft. Cass, although 20 were too sick to travel.[ccxl] The use of a Tennessee commander at a Georgia post all but confirms that Dorsey left his command abruptly.

Construction. The records found to this point do not include any information about possible construction at Ft. Newnan. The proper name of the post, however, indicates that it was fortified, and since the company assigned to the post was mounted, we can also assume they built stables. The company may not have needed huts since they arrived after winter had passed, but at this point we have no way to confirm or deny the possibility. In light of the number of letters relating to supplies, we can assume the company had considerable storage facilities.

Supplies. Subsistence stores were shipped from Ft. Cass to Ft. Newnan as early as March, although we have no details regarding amounts or kinds.[ccxli] By late April, it was apparent that the post could not obtain adequate forage. Mays had been able to purchase only 1,600 bushels of corn, which came from a site some 30 miles away.[ccxlii] In early May, Mays had only 500 to 600 bushels or corn and scarcely more fodder, primarily because all forage in the area was purchased by John J. Field for Ft. Hetzel.[ccxliii]

The scarcity of forage in the area, which may have been the result of the long occupancy of the nearby mission as well as the tavern, confirmed the wisdom of linking the posts for the distribution of supplies.

In late June, Mays wrote that he had no invoice for the 1,070 pounds of iron he had received, an amount that seems extraordinarily high.[ccxliv] In preparation for the sale of the public stores at Ft. Newnan, Campbell wrote from Dahlonega on June 29 that he planned to arrive at Ft. Newnan on Wednesday, July 4.[ccxlv] The subsequent correspondence indicates that Ft. Newnan's occupancy lasted from March 1-July 4, or no more than four months.

Prisoners. Other than the July 2 report from Capt. Dodson that he had arrived at Ft. Newnan to convey prisoners to Ft. Cass, no documentation has been found of the number of Cherokees removed by Dorsey's company.

Encampment at Chastain's (Blue Ridge, Union County)

To this point, the most useful material has been found in microfilm copies of papers relating to Cherokee removal. Originally from various collections in the National Archives, the papers have been combined into one record group (393) and are available on film at the National Archives Records Administration in East Point, Georgia. In addition, information about the location of Chastain's can be found in the cartographic branch of the National Archives. The proximity of Benjamin Chastain's home to the North Carolina border resulted in the location of his home on the survey maps made by the North Carolina troops in preparation for removal. North Carolina archaeologist Brett Riggs has interpreted the militia maps and places Chastain's in or near Garren Cove on the east side of the Toccoa River. In 1925, construction began on a dam across the Toccoa, which was completed in 1930. Lake Blue Ridge was formed by the dam and inundated the site where Chastain lived.

The encampment at Chastain's raises so many questions that the absence of records about the post has proven particularly frustrating. It seems the post's establishment was not initially planned. No mention was made of northeast Georgia until late May when other companies were already underway with their collection of prisoners. The assignment of three companies to Chastain's indicates the expectation of a high number of prisoners, yet the late assignment and failure of command suggest a lack of attention about their capture. The delayed arrival of Gen. Eustis to his command at Ft. Butler exacerbated the problems since no one was sufficiently near to monitor the post's establishment. Most puzzling of all was the behavior of and toward the commander, Lt. Col. Benjamin Camp, whose leadership and discipline failed from the very beginning. Yet he was allowed to pass from Ft. Buffington to Ft. Floyd and on to Union County, with complaints following him along the route. Although he resigned his commission, it is surprising that he did not face a court martial. The discovery of additional papers, particularly those of Gen. Eustis, will be a welcome addition to this body of literature about the removal of Indians from Chastain's.

Military Occupation. The earliest mention of a post at Chastain's occurred on May 11, 1838 when orders were sent from Ft. Cass for the disposition of Georgia regiments about to be mustered into service. From the first companies received, an unnamed lieutenant colonel and three companies were ordered to a post "near Chastain's in Union County."[ccxlvi] The infantry companies, one of which was commanded by Capt. John W. Fowler of DeKalb County, were marching from Ft. Buffington in Cherokee County (where they obtained their arms?) to Chastain's in then, Union County. Their probable route was from Canton to Dahlonega (by way of Ft. Campbell), then to Ft. Hetzel in Ellijay and on to Chastain's. By the end of May, Capt. Peake's company of Tennessee Volunteers was stationed at Chastain's awaiting the arrival of the three Georgia companies.[ccxlvii]

When Lt. Hetzel notified V. M. Campbell of his responsibility for the post at Chastain's, he noted that Gov. Gilmer would appoint the new post's quartermaster. Campbell's job was to instruct and furnish him with the necessary funds.[ccxlviii] An early June letter identifies the new quartermaster as A.P. Bush, who was, according to Campbell, inexperienced.[ccxlix] In the same week, another letter identifies the commander of the three companies as Lt. Col. Camp.[ccl]

The first sign of trouble appears in the records in early June when quartermaster Bush wrote that the commander was drunk, absent half the time, unable to command, and had so offended the soldiers at Ft. Buffington that they had "presented their muskets at him." He also pointed out that the companies did not march until the middle of the day and had already run out of rations.[ccli] The day after Bush complained to Col. Turk, quartermaster Campbell reported that he anticipated considerable trouble from the companies because Bush was inexperienced and both the officers and the men were "as rough and uncouth a set" as he had even seen.[cclii]

As soon as Floyd learned about the militia's behavior, he ordered Col. Turk to lead a cavalry party to pursue and arrest Camp. Meanwhile, Gen. Scott also was informed. He instructed Floyd to turn the matter over to Eustis at Ft. Butler.[ccliii] By mid-June, Col. Camp resigned his commission and returned home, leaving the three companies at Chastain's under the command of Maj. Kemp.[ccliv] On June 17, Eustis ordered two of the three companies to Ft. Wool and the following day he proposed sending Capt. Peake back to Chastain's to relieve the third.[cclv]

Construction. No mention of construction was found in any of the records. It is unlikely Peake constructed anything of substance since his assignment was temporary. The late arrival of the three Georgia companies makes the construction of barracks unlikely and the fact that they were infantry companies rendered stables unnecessary. Storage facilities would have been necessary unless the companies utilized buildings at Chastain's.

Supplies. The quartermaster department at Chastain's was put under the supervision of Ft. Floyd's V.M. Campbell, but in the review of correspondence from the quartermaster's department, no records of supply shipments have emerged. On the other hand, in early June, Eustis notified Lt. Col. Worth that 60 days' rations for three companies had been sent to the post.[cclvi] The delivery may have been in response to Bush's complaint that the companies had run out of rations by the time they reached Dahlonega.

Prisoners. No record has been found of prisoners taken by the companies at Chastain's.

Fort Hoskins (Springplace, Murray County)

Useful information about Ft. Hoskins was gathered from the National Archives microfilmed records related to Cherokee removal (East Point, Georgia) and the National Archives records of the quartermaster's department (Washington, D.C.). In addition, the early 1830s occupation by the Georgia Guard of a post at Spring Place (as it was then spelled) is well documented in the governor's correspondence at the Georgia Department of Archives and History. Although it is not known whether any connection exists between the two posts, a better understanding of each will benefit the effort to interpret this period of Cherokee history. Deed books in the Murray County courthouse, Chatsworth, are relatively complete for the removal era and research will continue in these records for information about property transfers that may contain references to the fort. As with Ft. Gilmer, which was also in Murray County, the county history compiled under the direction of Tim Howard provides useful data for the context of Cherokee removal.

Tim Howard informed us that the site of Ft. Hoskins was once thought to be near Highway 225 but stated that archaeologists working on the road found no traces of it. Howard and contract archaeologist Ron Hobgood then decided the site might be further east, nearer a branch, on property owned by Virginia and Randall Richards. For many years local citizens thought some removal soldiers were buried on the property, a possibility that reinforced the selection of the site. Unfortunately, no data has emerged regarding deaths of soldiers stationed at Ft. Hoskins, and Hobgood's work was promising but inconclusive. Fortunately, the Richards are supportive of additional work and interested in locating the site.

Spring Place Mission and School. Named by the Moravian missionaries who established the first permanent mission among the Cherokees in 1801, Spring Place was a small settlement in what is now west-central Murray County in the Great Valley of the Appalachian Plateau. The modern community of Springplace is just northeast of the mission site. When the Federal Road was run it passed in front of the mission, which helped make the site a stopping place for Cherokees, Creeks, and whites of varied denominations and political persuasions. James Vann's home stood about a mile away and, as a result, the mission became even more prominent in Cherokee life and the missionaries became well informed about Cherokee politics.

The mission and school were closed in January, 1833, when whites arrived to claim their property drawn in the state lottery of Cherokee lands. The following year, Springplace was incorporated as the county seat of Murray, which had been created in 1832. The first county elections took place in the homes of white settlers at Springplace and New Echota.

Earlier Military Stations. Two military camps operated in Murray County prior to the 1838 removal, which has added to the confusion about removal forts. One was Camp Benton at Spring Place. Col. William N. Bishop of the Georgia Guard (or Georgia Rangers) obtained the mission property by purchasing it from lottery winners, and he renamed the facility Camp Benton. Bishop used the station as his headquarters at least until July, 1836. Gen. John E. Wool assumed command of the Army of East Tennessee and the Cherokee Nation at that time and ordered an explanation of why a company was stationed at Spring Place.[cclvii] Under the command of Charles H. Nelson, Bishop and his company of approximately 36 men scoured the Cherokee Nation in Georgia, arrested Cherokees and whites for various offences, spied on the activities of suspects, and maintained frequent communication with the governor, federal agents, and members of the Treaty Party. In 1835, Bishop removed the Cherokee Nation's printing press, which has never been recovered.

The state provided the Guard with weapons and perhaps other supplies as well. At one point, Bishop had under guard Walter S. Adair, Thomas Taylor, missionary James Trott, and Elijah Hicks because they were appointed by John Ross to value Cherokee improvements.[cclviii] In November 1835, the Guard gained their greatest notoriety by arresting, in Tennessee, Chief John Ross and author John Howard Payne. Since Payne was a national figure, the Guard's actions caused the state of Georgia considerable embarrassment.

In the summer of 1836, Cherokee agent Cornelius D. Terhune wrote the governor with objections to the behavior of Bishop's company toward the Indians. "They have taken them up without due process," he wrote, "retained them in chains, for days and weeks together, and caused them to perform all the drudgeries of the camps, and then turned them loose for want of any evedence [sic] against them, and in some instances, without even attempting to prossicute [sic] them."[cclix]

In addition to the conflation of Camp Benton with the removal stockades, the participation of another militia volunteer named Bishop has proved confusing. Capt. Absalom B. Bishop, William's brother, commanded a company of the Highland Battalion during removal. Absalom served previously as a private in William's company, and research has not yet documented the post, if any, of Absalom Bishop's company. The Highland Battalion was commanded by Maj. Charles H. Nelson, who was responsible for the arrest and mistreatment of Samuel Worcester and the other Georgia missionaries in 1831. The missionaries were imprisoned at Camp Gilmer at Scudder's, also in Murray County.[cclx]

Military Occupation. Inconsistency and perhaps confusion prevailed regarding the companies ordered to Spring Place. Just as in Dahlonega, dissension flourished over which citizens would be recognized as the true militia. In the winter of 1838, a new militia company was commanded by R. H. S. Buchanan, who told the governor that competition between the Bishop and anti-Bishop forces in the county had become something of a contest.[cclxi] Two weeks later, another new militia company (commanded by James Sample) reported to the governor.[cclxii] The following month, Absalom Bishop replied to a criticism by the governor regarding his long-established militia company.[cclxiii]

Although the records indicate the existence of these three companies by early March, one Richard Butler felt obliged to remind the governor of the "importance of stationing a company here." Apparently unaware that Spring Place was more than adequately defended, Butler felt particularly threatened by the Indians of Coosawattee.[cclxiv] By the end of March, plans were made for Capt. Hammond (Hamilton?) Garmany of Gwinnett County to establish a post at Spring Place.[cclxv] Thereafter, correspondence reveals that Capt. Thomas S. Jones of Newton County actually became the commander of a single mounted company at Spring Place.[cclxvi] His quartermaster was R. Agnew.[cclxvii]

Perhaps the various citizens seeking recognition as militia members or the possible lack of experience of Capt. Jones shaped the conflict that became evident following the removal of prisoners. On June 6, Floyd reported to Scott that there had been one case of mutiny at Ft. Hoskins and several cases of insubordination.[cclxviii] Floyd emphasized that the cases would "not pass unpunished" and we can hope that additional research in the court martial records will provide the missing details. On June 30, Capt. Jones's company arrived at New Echota for mustering out.[cclxix]

Construction. The post at Spring Place was referred to as a camp or station until the end of May, at which time it was called Ft. Hoskins, likely in honor of Lt. Charles Hoskins of the Fourth Artillery Company.[cclxx] We assume that Capt. Jones and his company fortified their post by that time. Since the post was not occupied in winter months, it is likely the company slept in tents rather than barracks. As a mounted company, the men needed to stable their horses either at the post or in town. If the post was close to the growing community of Springplace, the company could have used public stables, but since there are no invoices in the records for stabling horses, we can infer that the company built stables. Jones's invoice for ovens and pots indicates the construction of brick ovens or fire pits.[cclxxi]

The records hint that Ft. Hoskins may have been the center for hospital supplies. In early May, a wagon arrived "to deliver medicine and hospital supplies from here to Dahlonega." The following week, the Dahlonega quartermaster complained that he had not received the hospital supplies because the Hoskins quartermaster had been absent when the wagon came by.[cclxxii] If Hoskins indeed served as hospital store, additional construction would have resulted.

Supplies. By the end of March, Lt. A. Cox at New Echota was responsible for the quartermaster department at the Spring Place post. In addition to Ft. Wool, Cox's other posts were Ft. Buffington (Canton), Ft. Cumming (Lafayette), and the encampment at Cedar Town (Paulding County).[cclxxiii] Although the occupation records are sparse, the quartermasters' accounts indicate that Spring Place was fully occupied by March 31, when the first bills of lading for the transport of subsistence supplies arrived.[cclxxiv] Subsequent bills arrived on April 4 and 24, May 1, and May 8.[cclxxv] The 300 pounds of salt for the post matches the amount sent to Ft. Gilmer.

The proximity of Ft. Hoskins to vendors is indicated by the lack of concern about additional corn and fodder to feed the horses. On May 1, according to the records, neither was on hand at the post, but 1,200 bushels of corn and 10,000 bundles of fodder were said to be obtainable.[cclxxvi] With three weeks yet to go before the commencement of the removal, the absence of corn and fodder for the horses seems irresponsible.

On June 17, plans were made for the disposition of all public property at Ft. Hoskins. According to Hetzel, the presence of Col. Cox at Ft. Hoskins would be indispensable. Hetzel's plan was for each post commander to give 6-8 days notice to the public, and schedule to auction for the day before the company left the post.[cclxxvii]

Prisoners. On May 30, Capt. Jones reported to Floyd that he had captured 79 Cherokees including 19 men, 24 women, and 36 children.[cclxxviii] The records located to this point give no details of the capture or of any subsequent efforts to locate prisoners. On June 9, however, Jones reported that 122 captives had been sent under escort from Spring Place directly to Ross's Landing. The relatively low number reinforces the assumption that life for Cherokees in the area was quite difficult between 1832 and 1838, and many chose to move to other communities.[cclxxix]

An unusual communication of June 2 is pertinent to Spring Place, though it may not have involved Ft. Hoskins. Removal Superintendent Nathaniel Smith wrote to Gen. Scott that he gave permission to Nancy Butler and her father, Toosawallaty, to leave the camps and return to their home at Spring Place in order to dispose of some of their property. "They left," he wrote, "among other things, 4 fine beds."[cclxxx] Smith's leniency regarding the travels of Cherokee prisoners displeased Floyd, who considered the return of Cherokees to the state for any reason was a bad precedent and seriously undermined the effort of removal.

Fort Campbell (Blaine, Forsythe County)

Of the few located sources with information about Ft. Campbell, the most useful was the quartermaster's reports at the National Archives in Washington, the collection of Cherokee removal records at the National Archives Records Administration in East Point, Georgia, and the correspondence of Gov. Gilmer housed at the Georgia Department of Archives and History. Ft. Campbell was in the Middle Military District commanded by Gen. Eustis. As with other Georgia posts east of Ft. Wool, data remains limited.

Two residents of Forsyth County are considered particularly knowledgeable about Cherokee history, county historian Don Shadburn and Cherokee descendent Lucian Lamar Sneed. Both believe Ft. Campbell was located at the junction of Forsyth, Lumpkin, and Cherokee counties, placing it just west of Scudder's and on the north side of the Federal Road (Illustration 19. Possible location of Fort Campbell).

Scudder's, Camp Eaton, and Camp Gilmer. Jacob Scudder owned a stand on the Federal Road that played a part in the military history of the Cherokee Nation in Georgia prior to removal. In late May, 1830, Gov. George Gilmer requested help from the federal

Illustration 19. Possible location of Fort Campbell.

government in protecting the gold mines that were discovered in the late 1820s. With the approval of President Jackson, the Secretary of War sent two companies of the 4th regiment to establish a post at a strategic location in the Cherokee Nation. Capt. Francis Brady's company arrived soon after and constructed a fort of logs on a hill near Scudder's inn. The post included a blacksmith shop, barracks, stables, and buildings for storage and other purposes. The location of Camp Eaton, as it was called, is identified on the 1832 survey maps on lots 302, 202, 246, and 347. The withdrawal of federal troops began in October of the same year.[cclxxxi]

In December, Scudder replied to Gilmer's request to station the Georgia Guard at Camp Eaton and included a brief description of the post. There were eight rooms in a line occupying 20 square feet. Four rooms lacked floors and parts of a chimney, but planks for the floors were left in Scudder's charge. Several outbuildings remained, some of which contained corn and fodder that Scudder purchased from the departing quartermaster. Apparently, there was also a guardhouse.[cclxxxii]

In January 1831, militia Col. John W. A. Sanford and his subaltern, Col. Charles H. Nelson, arrived with voluntary recruits and began repairing the barracks. The Georgia Guard remained at the renamed Camp Gilmer until the following October, and Scudder was under contract to supply their provisions. While stationed at Camp Gilmer, the Guard's most notorious act was the arrest and temporary confinement of missionaries Elizur Butler and Samuel Worcester.[cclxxxiii] Gov. George Gilmer later described Nelson as "a man of lawless violence."[cclxxxiv]

Jacob Scudder was a white man who moved with his wife and toddler son into the Cherokee Nation around 1815. He had just been discharged from service in the War of 1812, where he served in the company commanded by Nehemiah Garrison, who was later associated with the possible location of Ft. Buffington. Scudder carried on an active trade with Indians and whites at his stand near the crossing of the Alabama and Federal Roads in the Hightower community. In 1827, he was named postmaster. After several years of pressure from the Cherokee Nation, which objected to the competition from white-owned businesses, Scudder moved to the east of Hightower, but remained in the Cherokee Nation.[cclxxxv]

Following the 1831 survey of Cherokee lands and the 1832 creation of Forsyth County, elections were held in Scudder's home for the new representatives to the Georgia General Assembly, and he was elected to the Georgia Senate. The state subsequently employed him to identify land lots abandoned by Indians and to survey Floyd County in the Cherokee Nation. By the end of his life, Scudder was one of the largest landowners and slaveholders in Forsyth County. His son, Alfred, married a woman of Cherokee descent in 1833, making Alfred, as well as his children, citizens of the Cherokee Nation.[cclxxxvi] In short, Jacob Scudder and his public stop would have been well known among whites as well as Cherokees at the time of removal. Establishing a post very near his stand would have been sensible, and would have provided the quartermaster with a resource when needed.

Camp Eaton/Gilmer and Scudder's remain important to the history of Indian removal for several reasons. Many sources mistakenly list Camp Eaton or Camp Gilmer as a removal stockade. Others confuse Camp Gilmer in Forsyth County with Fort Gilmer in Murray County, miss-identifying both the date and the facility. Some sources refer to Fort Eaton or even Fort Scudder. Trail of Tears markers placed at the appropriate sites in Georgia will be an invaluable source of education for all.

Scudder's inn was in the Hickory Log District of the Cherokee Nation, in the upper Piedmont physiographic province between the Chattahoochee and the Etowah rivers. Local Cherokees lived on river tributaries including Settendown (sometimes spelled Setting or Sitting Down), Baldridge, Young Deer, Vickery, and Big Creeks. Nearby Cherokee communities included Hightower, Frogtown, and Ducktown. In anticipation of removal, Capt. James Word reported that some 500 Cherokees lived within "the limits" of Ft. Campbell, usually considered a ten-mile radius.[cclxxxvii] With proximity to the Federal and Alabama Roads as well as major water routes, Hightower attracted a number of grog shops at the time of removal. Capt. Word reported that several persons were keeping "their little shops" where they sold "intoxicating liquor" to the Indians as well as "powder and lead."[cclxxxviii]

Military Occupation. In early April, Lt. Mackay notified Lt. Hetzel that Capt. Jones was to be mustered in at New Echota and sent to Scudder's, but Jones then disappears from the post's records (although he may be the same Thomas S. Jones who was commander at Ft. Hoskins, Spring Place, Murray County).[cclxxxix] By mid-May, Capt. James A. Word of Campbell County was in command of the mounted company of 74 men stationed at Ft. Campbell.[ccxc] It is likely the post, like the county, was named for Duncan G. Campbell, who negotiated the 1825 Treaty of Indian Springs ceding all Creek land in Georgia. Whether the company at the post was aware of the irony or intended it cannot be known.

A single letter from Word to James Mackay contains an unusual amount of data about his company, the process of removal, and the environs. When Word traveled to the surrounding Cherokee towns to read Gen. Scott's address to resident Cherokees, he was accompanied by a Cherokee named Charles Crittenden, who served as his interpreter. His two lieutenants, Berry L. Watts (or Waits) and Martin D. Rogers, each visited one of the towns on behalf of Word.[ccxci] On June 9, Rogers escorted the prisoners to Ft. Wool and on to Ross's Landing, and the company returned to New Echota on June 30 for payment and mustering out.[ccxcii]

In his letter, written a few days before collecting prisoners, Word requested that a physician be assigned to his company because of the serious illness of one of his men. If physicians were unavailable, he wrote, he could hire one at once who was well qualified and apparently known to his company. Concerned that the soldier was dying, Word anticipated the arrival of his father and requested permission for the father to take his son home.[ccxciii] The sick soldier's name is not given.

In early May, Lt. Hetzel appointed R. F. Hilbourn as quartermaster for Ft. Campbell.[ccxciv] Later in the month, Word's letter identified two other individuals in the company who were assigned special jobs. He detailed David D.

Smith to serve as quartermaster sergeant and John Carlton to act as company sergeant.[ccxcv] With this information, we know more about the responsibilities of specific individuals in Word's company than in any others.

Construction. Military correspondence in early April proposed the establishment of a post at or near Scudder's. By May 1, the post was referred to by its proper name, implying that it was fortified. On May 20, however, Word wrote that he had "not yet completed only about one [fourth?] of the picket work" because he had lacked adequate tools until recently. With tools in hand, he hoped to complete it in 10-12 days, which obviously was a period that extended beyond the capture of prisoners.[ccxcvi] Since earlier correspondence at Ft. Wool had included orders for construction tools for company commanders, Word's lack of tools may indicate a breakdown of efficiency in the late stages of preparation for removal. Unless he was utilizing buildings at Scudder's, Word would have needed to construct storage facilities, barracks, stables, and cooking facilities in a brief period.

Supplies. Little forage was available for purchase in the area around Ft. Campbell. On May 1, Word had only 200 bushels of corn and 550 bundles of fodder. The quartermaster estimated that he could probably acquire 4,000 bushels of corn, but no bundles of fodder. The only other post in Georgia unlikely to obtain fodder was Ft. Floyd.[ccxcvii] No other supply records for Ft. Campbell have been found.

Prisoners. In mid-June, Word reported that his company had worked five days to capture about 200 Indians "without loss of life or fire of gun." When adequate wagons and teams became available, he sent the prisoners with their baggage on to Ross's Landing. He subsequently captured ten more individuals and sent them to New Echota. A few Indians in his area had "certificates" allowing them to remain.[ccxcviii] These likely included the Rogers family on the Chattahoochee River, the younger Scudder and his family, the Cherokee family of Thomas Cordery, the George Waters family, George Welch and his family, and the Lewis Blackburn family.[ccxcix] Passes may also have been issued to Indians too sick or elderly to move.

Fort Cumming (Lafayette, Walker County)

Sources for Ft. Cumming in Lafayette were varied and included the National Archives records of the quartermaster's department, the governors' correspondence at the Georgia Department of Archives and History, the combined records of Cherokee removal on microfilm at the National Archives Records Administration, and the Special Collections Department of the Woodruff Library at Emory University, Atlanta. Emory houses the records of Benjamin T. Watkins, commander of a company of Georgia infantrymen stationed at Ft. Cumming. Watkins was previously unknown in the story of Ft. Cumming, and the discovery of his papers has added immeasurably to our understanding of events at the site.

Walker County citizens are heir to a long tradition of interest in Native Americans in general and the removal of the Cherokees in particular. In 1915, Mrs. Frances Park Stiles, long-time historian for the William Marsh chapter of the Daughters of the American Revolution, wrote an article about removal for the *Walker County Messenger*. The article includes the following description of the fort in Lafayette:

The stockade was a large enclosure of upright logs; the trenches where the logs were placed can still be plainly seen. There was a rifle tower in each corner after the manner of frontier posts, post holes were formed by sawing flared notches in the logs before they were put in the buildings. On the inside of the tower the port holes were eight or ten inches across, thus allowing room for changing the course of the rifle fire.[ccc]

Stiles does not cite sources, but she does name one local citizen who remembered "seeing the old fort when it was about half rotted down." She identifies the fort site as "on the hill just west of the Big Spring where the city of Lafayette, Ga., gets its water supply." According to Stiles, the watchtower stood on the hill adjacent to and west of the spring.[ccci]

The fort description by Stiles has informed the thinking of almost everyone in Georgia who is interested in the Trail of Tears. It has been repeated in numerous publications, often without credit to Stiles. Congruent with images of frontier posts, it has provided illustrators with enough detail to enable them to sketch removal posts with considerable confidence. Verifying, amending, or refuting the description remains a goal of this research.

In addition to Stiles' work, the late Doris Hetzler of Lafayette accumulated papers related to Cherokee life and removal, and her collection is housed in the Cherokee Regional Library in Lafayette. A review of the Hetzler collection, however, produced no additional information. In 1972, James Alfred Sartain published a *History of Walker County Georgia* that includes descriptions of removal activities in Walker County. Sartain acknowledged that his "comprehensive review" of Cherokee removal was copied or paraphrased from various other accounts and that not all the events included actually took place in Walker County. Although not helpful regarding the Cherokee deportation, Sartain's work has helped identify settlements and trails that were surely important during the process

Contemporary residents of the area have been particularly supportive of further research. Special mention should be made of Clayton Bell, president of the Walker County Historical Society, and Dr. David Boyle of Dalton College, both of who have been generous with time and tips for further research. Boyle and I continue a genial disagreement about the post's name. Boyle accepts the common wisdom that the post honors the missionary David B. Cumming, who was appointed as an itinerant in 1836 by the Holston (Tennessee) Methodist Conference. Cumming's mission circuit included Georgia and he requested reassignment to Arkansas in order to accompany the Cherokees when they were removed.[cccii] I have proposed a Georgia war hero, Col. William Cumming, for whom the town of Cumming, Georgia is named, as a more likely honoree. My idea derives from the fact that no other post in Georgia was named for a friend of the Indians, and most were named for someone in the military or in Georgia politics. Until more records are located, resolution of this particular disagreement remains unfulfilled.

A recent conversation with Tennessee chapter member Vicki Rozema pointed to another source of information about Cherokees in the area of Lafayette. Rozema was told that the records of the Peavine Baptist Church include the information that Cherokee prisoners were housed in the original church while waiting to be moved from Georgia to Tennessee. Efforts to contact the church are ongoing.

A state historical marker, which is now in disrepair, stands near the purported site of the post (Illustration 20. Fort Cumming historical marker). It replaced a boulder with a small bronze marker placed at the site by the Marsh chapter some years before 1935 and subsequently stolen.

Illustration 20. Fort Cumming historical marker.

Walker County was carved out of Murray County in 1833, shortly after the Cherokee land survey. The county included Rossville and the last Georgia home of John Ross, Crawfish Town on Peavine Creek (where George Lowrey lived) and an original Cherokee courthouse, Strawberry on the Armuchee River, Dogwood on Chickamauga Creek (home of Charles Hicks), Chestnut Town on Peavine Creek, Lookout Mountain Town on Lookout Creek, Duck Town on Duck Creek in the Chattooga Valley, and White Oak Town on Spring Creek. Crawfish Town is now called Chickamauga.

Lying in the northwest portion of Georgia, the county is primarily in the Ridge and Valley physiographic province, though its western edge is part of the Appalachian Plateau. The Alabama Road (later the Brainerd Road) followed the path of least resistance in a northeast-southwest direction. When the Cherokees divided their nation into districts, the area that became Walker County was in the Chickamauga District. In 1836, the name of the town of Chattooga was changed to Lafayette, now spelled LaFayette.

Military Occupation. The military occupation of Lafayette began prior to the Cherokee removal crisis and apparently included Samuel Farris (also spelled Farriss, Farish, and others), who later commanded the removal company. In March, 1838, Farris certified that he had employed one James Caldwell to take charge of the "military post at the courthouse" to guard the munitions "in the late Creek campaign."[ccciii] Lafayette thus joins Canton and Dahlonega as places where munitions were stored in the courthouses a year or two prior to Cherokee removal. The presence of munitions implies the establishment of militia companies and a degree of state organization. It also serves as another indicator of conditions the Cherokees faced and the certainty of their removal following the signing of the treaty.

In 1836, Farris commanded more than 100 men in the 45th company of the Georgia Militia.[ccciv] Apparently he was then mustered out, and in 1838 raised another company of approximately 75 men for Lindsey's Georgia Mounted Militia.[cccv] Little correspondence exists between the two militia lists, with perhaps fewer than five men serving in both companies.

In March 1838, Quartermaster Hetzel anticipated Farris's mustering in with his new company of mounted volunteers.[cccvi] Farris then received orders to proceed to his hometown of Lafayette, and by April 17, was at his post.[cccvii] His quartermaster, J. M. Collon, reported to Col. Cox at New Echota and received post supplies from him.[cccviii] The May 17, 1838 list of volunteer posts in the Cherokee Nation confirms that one mounted company was stationed at Ft. Cumming.[cccix]

Although Farris generally is recognized as commander at Ft. Cumming, another militia captain also held a position of responsibility and actually assumed command for a brief period. On May 7, 1838, Benjamin T. Watkins of Campbell County was ordered by the governor to serve as captain of a company of drafted men and report to New Echota.[cccx] Over the next several days, Watkins received camp and garrison equipage for 75 men and apparently was directed to Ft. Cumming.[cccxi]

On June 9, Floyd learned that Farris was absent without leave and planned to arrest him when he returned to his post.[cccxii] As problems developed at Ft. Cumming in Farris's absence, Watkins assumed command. On June 9, Watkins wrote that he had arrested Lewis W. Fretwell of the horse company for intoxication, abusive language "for the purpose of riot," rioting, disrespectful language to officers and men, and attempted murder. As post commander, Watkins requested instructions from Floyd regarding discipline as well as the resolution of a complaint about one of the post's horses.[cccxiii] The following week, Floyd officially appointed Watkins as commander during the period of Farris's arrest.[cccxiv] Since most of the prisoners had been sent from Ft. Cumming by June 9, it seems likely that Farris left the post at that time and put Watkins in charge. On June 18, Watkins was ordered to headquarters, presumably for discharge.[cccxv] His absence from all Ft. Cumming records other than his own serves as a caution for researchers at every level.

Floyd did arrest Farris, but subsequently accepted the explanation for his absence and restored him to office.[cccxvi] In the interval, Farris also had to mollify Gov. Gilmer, whose office complained that Farris had never reported the details of his company's organization.[cccxvii] By early July, Farris was out of trouble and in command. He arrived with his company at New Echota on July 5, and was mustered out of service the following day.[cccxviii]

Construction. Throughout March and April, references were made to the post in Lafayette or Walker County. As late as May 5, quartermaster Collon's return address was simply "Lafayette." On May 11, however, the records begin to refer to Ft. Cumming.[cccxix] Although no records refer to post construction, we can assume that by Mid-May the post included a stockade and stables for the horses of the mounted men. We can also infer the construction of barracks since the camp and garrison lists include no more than a few tents. Storage facilities also were necessary for corn and fodder, weapons, equipment, and food rations for the 150 men and several hundred prisoners.

Although no descriptions of the fort have been located in the research to this point, several documents refer to the fort as such. In his diary of the removal, missionary Daniel Butrick mourns the imprisonment of hundreds of Cherokees in a fort near Lafayette Courthouse.[cccxx] John Looking was one of them. On March 2, 1842, Looking submitted his claim for lost property. He stated that, "troops took me and put me into a fort near Walker Court House in Georgia."[cccxxi] Years later, an account of the Civil War battle around Lafayette included the statement that federal troops entered the town "back of the old fort."[cccxxii]

Supplies. Subsistence supplies were sent to the post as early as April 4, 1838, which may provide an approximate date for Farris's arrival.[cccxxiii] Quartermaster Collon visited before the company arrived and arranged for the delivery of 1,200 bushels of corn.[cccxxiv] By the first of May, however, the post was relatively low on corn (200 bushels) and had no fodder at all. A confident Collon estimated that he could

obtain 3,000 bushels of corn and 10,000 bundles of fodder.[cccxxv]

Rations for the companies and prisoners caused Collon some concern since his stilyards apparently did not weigh accurately. He complained that the number of pieces of bacon he received was correct but their weight fell 193 pounds short.[cccxxvi] No other mention of food for the post was found in the quartermaster's records.

Watkins's records include lists of equipment distributed to his company that give a sense of the vast amount of material purchased and used during the removal. Watkins's company received frying pans, tin pans, camp kettles, tin buckets, tea kettles, and spiders for their daily subsistence.[cccxxvii] Cox also provided Watkins with one wall tent and fly, seven common tents, six axes, and four spades.[cccxxviii] Munitions included muskets, bayonets with straps and scabbards, cartridge boxes and straps, bell plates, wipers, and ball screws.[cccxxix] Watkins even returned nine deficient muskets to New Echota.[cccxxx] He certified that all supplies were necessary for the company and all had been procured at the lowest prices.[cccxxxi] On June 17, plans were conveyed for the sale of all remaining public property at Ft. Cumming.[cccxxxii]

Prisoners. Perhaps as many as 500 Indians were collected at Ft. Cumming and sent to Ross's Landing. Under orders of Winfield Scott they were considered prisoners of war, though no resistance had been encountered.[cccxxxiii] Daniel Butrick provided an account of the roundup:

> Found our dear brother Epenetus Aehaia and his wife and children among prisoners. On the 28th May they spent the night at Dogwood Flat and the next day heard that soldiers were rounding up Ga Cherokees. They were taken by a company of soldiers and driven to a fort near Lafayette Courthouse, kept with about 500 others for 10 days and driven to the

camps. While at the fort the whole company of 500 resolved to have nothing to do with the treaty money.[cccxxxiv]

On June 9, Floyd wrote that 469 Indians were escorted from Ft. Cumming to Ross's Landing.[cccxxxv] That same day, a letter from the commander at Ft. Poinsett conveyed a surprising degree of humaneness in a request to send all remaining prisoners from Ft. Cumming because they were part of families already in the internment camps.[cccxxxvi] At that time, some 60-70 Indians remained at the post and still more were arriving. Watkins reported to Floyd that a Cherokee named Aaron Wilkiman hoped to remain at home until he was paid a debt owed him by a white man named Thomas York.[cccxxxvii] On June 10, Watkins ordered Lt. Wood to detail from his company one sergeant, one corporal, and 18 privates to aid in escorting prisoners the following day. He omitted mention of Wilkiman and his debt.[cccxxxviii]

Fort Means (Kingston, Floyd County)

Information about Ft. Means was gathered primarily from the collected records of Cherokee removal on microfilm at the National Archives Records Administration in East Point, Georgia. A few relevant records were found in the National Archives records of the quartermaster department in Washington, D.C., and in the correspondence of Gov. George Gilmer located at the Georgia Department of Archives and History, Atlanta.

Trail of Tears state chapter members J. B. Tate and Doug Mabry undertook most of the research about Ft. Means and located deeds in the Floyd and Bartow County courthouses that were congruent with distances from the post mentioned by Capt. Means. As a result of the Means records and the work of Mabry and Tate, we have an excellent chance to pinpoint the post's location. Mabry's report and supporting documents are attached to the Ft. Means site report.

Military Occupation. The military occupation of Ft. Means was initiated by Gilmer in March 1838, when he ordered John Means of Walton County into service. Means served in the Seminole War (likely under Nelson) and was considered suitable for posting at Dahlonega.[cccxxxix] By early April, however, he was directed to establish a post "in Floyd County, Georgia near the dividing line between it and Cass County and also near the Hightower [Etowah] River."[cccxl] It may be that Means's military experience qualified him to establish a post in the midst of the prominent white planters who had claimed and purchased sizeable land lots along the Etowah River in Floyd County.

In mid-April, Means wrote Gilmer that he had mustered into service at New Echota with 65 privates and three subalterns, and received orders from Lindsay to proceed to the Hightower (Etowah) River near the line of Floyd and Cass in Floyd County.[cccxli] The military orders of May 11 and 17 confirm that one mounted company was stationed at Ft. Means, Floyd County, 88 miles from the Cherokee Agency in Tennessee, and a second company was ordered to proceed there. [cccxlii] The company was commanded by Capt. F. W. Cook of Oglethorpe County, and included a private who was either scared senseless or bloodthirsty, or both.

Pvt. Frances M. Cuthbert earned the miserable distinction of having killed a Cherokee in the process of removal. The records claim the Indian was killed while trying to escape, but the act motivated Floyd to issue orders forbidding the use of arms except when Indians resisted "with deadly weapons."[cccxliii] Cuthbert was exonerated.

It is noteworthy that the papers of Capt. Benjamin Watkins, who was stationed at Ft. Cumming, contain an invoice for equipment issued to Capt. Cook on May 14. The reason Watkins had an invoice for Cook's company has not been determined, but it may be that Cook moved from Ft. Cumming to Ft. Means or the reverse. More information about the movement of troops to different posts will shed light on the organization and disorganization of removal, the number of Georgians who participated as militia soldiers, the degree of communication between the posts, and the connection between Georgians and Cherokees removed from the state.

On June 30, Means arrived at New Echota with his company, with plans to muster out as soon as the paymaster paid them for their work.[cccxliv]

Construction. The records of the fortification at Means are more complete than for most posts in Georgia. On April 15, Means wrote Gilmer that he had selected his position and commenced work.[cccxlv] In one week he completed the fort except for hanging the gate, and almost finished the blockhouse.[cccxlvi] Records indicate that a blockhouse was built at Ft. Wool, and with the information that Means included, we might assume blockhouses were built at every post. As with other posts, it is likely that the companies at Ft. Means also built stables for the horses and storage facilities for the supplies. It may not have been necessary to construct barracks since the occupation was brief and began in early spring, but no conclusions can be reached until documentation of the supplies used at the post can be located.

Supplies. Supplies were sent to the post as soon as Means was ordered to Floyd County. The quartermaster was assigned to Cox's division, and Cox received the bill for the transport of supplies to Means on April 4.[cccxlvii] On May 1, the quartermaster reported 150 bushels corn and no fodder at the post, but he estimated that he could obtain 3,000 bushels of corn, and 10,000 bundles of fodder at reasonable prices.[cccxlviii] No additional information about supplies for Ft. Means was found other than the plan for disposing of public stores, which was conveyed on June 17. As with other posts, the commander was ordered to give six-to-eight days' notice for people to assemble, and to set an auction date for one day prior to the departure of the troops. Col. Cox was ordered to supervise the sale in order to attend to the government's interests.[cccxlix]

Prisoners. Means's letter to Lindsay estimating the number of Indians living near his post contains unique information about site location. No other report contains both the number of miles from the post to the Indians' homes and the names of the white landowners who held the property. The letter states that 646 Indians lived within a 10-miles radius of Ft. Means, in cabins along the Etowah and Oostanaula Rivers and Euharlie Creek.[cccl]

Means apparently proceeded slowly to capture the Indians. Two days after the commencement of removal, he told Floyd he had successfully taken prisoners but he did not state the number.[cccli] On May 30, he reported that he had under guard 85 men, 85 women, and 83 children along with "7 negroes," for a total of 260 prisoners.[ccclii] The number almost doubled in the next week, and by June 9, Means had escorted to Ross's Landing 467 Cherokee captives.[cccliii]

In addition to the killing of a captive who had tried to escape, the prisoners from Ft. Means suffered an additional tragedy while they were camped at Ft. Wool. Floyd wrote to Scott that an Indian "of a party from Ft.

Means struck a soldier with a rock while in camp near this post." Floyd ordered the Indian seized and chained in the blockhouse at Ft. Wool."[ccccliv]

Cedar Town (Polk County)

Data about the encampment at Cedar Town (as it was then spelled) was located in the quartermasters' records in the National Archives, the governors' correspondence in the Georgia Department of Archives and History, and the microfilm collections of removal records at the National Archives Records Administration in East Point, Georgia. The Special Collections of the Hargrett Library at the University of Georgia contain the military records of Capt. Isaac S. Vincent, commander at Cedar Town, and those records have been copied to the on-line collection of Documents Relating to Southeastern Indians that is currently accessed through Galileo. Although the documents consistently refer to the camp at Cedar Town, they give no information about its specific location.

Three local contacts were particularly helpful: Kevin McAuliff of the North Georgia Regional Development Center in Dalton, Mike Wyatt of the Historic Preservation Committee in Cedartown, and Bill Blankenship, president of Ft. Mountain Preservation Services. McAuliff believes the encampment site was at Charley Town (also spelled Char le Town, Charlie Town) because a substantial number of whites lived in Cedar Town by the time of removal. All correspondence found for the encampment refers only to Cedar Town, but such identification may not be meaningful. It may, for example, refer to the post office location.

In 1898, a Dr. Charles K. Henderson wrote a history of Polk County in which he claimed that a company of U. S. troops "camped west of Cedartown on Big Cedar during the winter of 1837-38 to gather up the remnant of Indians which, refusing to go, had fled to the forest." He goes on to say that in the spring of 1838, approximately 200 Indians "were carried from Cedartown along the Rome Road to Gunter's Landing, now Guntersville on the Tennessee River, and from thence were sent to the far west." Although Henderson does not credit his sources, we cannot discount his narrative. [ccclv]

Cedar Town lay in the southernmost portion of the Cherokee Nation in Georgia, in the Etowah District, just east of the Alabama line. As the southernmost segment of the Great Valley of the Appalachian Plateau, the Cedar Town area was and is underlain by limestone, through which poured numerous springs. Cherokees and, later, whites settled along the Coosa River tributaries such as Cedar Creek. Big Spring on Cedar Creek was perhaps the largest natural limestone spring in the South.

Charley Town stood on Big Cedar Creek just north of Cedar Town. Henderson places Charley Town "south of Mr. Ake's once the homestead of Mr. Lazanus Battle," and states the town had "150 Indian huts built of pine poles and daubed inside and outside with mud."[ccclvi] The 1836 valuations do not support Henderson's description. Charle, apparently the town chief at the time of the evaluations, owned a log home with a piazza, a separate kitchen larger than his home, stables, a corn crib, peach trees, and 40 acres of improved land.[ccclvii] Other Cherokees on Cedar Creek lived in similarly comfortable homes that did not differ substantially from those of most white neighbors.

In 1842, many Cherokees made compensation claims for property taken from them on Cedar Creek. The claims of Daniel and Nancy Pumpkinpile, *Uk kwahle, Aka,Oo tah ne anter,* Henry Earbob, *Cah se ta kah, Con ah tane*, John Conahtane, Sally Mitchel, *Ah noo yah, and* Young Chicken are among the many dispossessed Cherokees who were forced from their Cedar Creek residences.[ccclviii] It is striking that most of the claimants refer to their removal by boat under escort of a government agent, which gives some credence to the Henderson account. The claim of Henry Earbob, for example, states that, "he lived on Cedar Creek and came to this country by water…." Young Chicken claimed he lived in Cedar Town and "came to this country with an agent of the Gen'l Govt by water."[ccclix] Future research into the detachment records may confirm these accounts, and Henderson's as well.

Following the 1832 lottery of Cherokee lands, Paulding County was created. On Boynton's 1838 map of Georgia, Cedar Town appears as the only settlement in Paulding and sits on the east side of Cedar Creek. According to Henderson, Ballenger Gravelly settled on Cedar Creek in 1834, and Martin Kelly developed a trade in whiskey and other goods sometime before 1837.[ccclx] By then, enough whites had migrated to the area to justify the establishment of the Cedar Town Academy. One of them was, by all accounts, an authentic troublemaker named John Witcher, whose military initiatives have confused efforts to identify the Cedar Town encampment site.

Capt. John Witcher raised a militia company in Paulding County in accordance with the Georgia General Assembly Act of 1837 that called for companies to protect the citizens and remove the Indians. That same year, one W. H. Adair complained to the governor that Cedar Town was "the only place in the County where there are any considerable settlement of Indians." Moreover, he stated, Cedar Town was the nearest "Cherokee village" to Creek country and many Cherokees had intermarried with their neighboring Creeks.[ccclxi] Soon after, Witcher urged the governor to call into service his mounted company of 43 men, and by April 1838, he had received his munitions from Capt. Buffington in Canton.[ccclxii]

Although the federal command under Maj. Payne was assigning troops to specific locations, Witcher apparently enjoyed the support of some local citizenry. In mid-May, Gen. Scott declined a request from a group of prominent white Cedar Town residents to muster in Witcher's company.[ccclxiii] Nonetheless, Witcher continued to act as leader of the Cedar Town militia. Agent Lacy Witcher (relationship unknown) complained to the governor that John Witcher and his company were often intoxicated, unfit for service, and antagonistic toward the Indians, who had remained friendly and peaceful. After John Witcher's company camped near Cedar Town and shot at passing Indians, many had moved away.[ccclxiv] Gilmer acknowledged that Witcher was serving in defiance of the state, but took no immediate action.[ccclxv]

When Floyd learned of the Cedar Town controversy, he promptly dispatched a staff officer to investigate and arrest Witcher if necessary.[ccclxvi] On June 18, Floyd accepted Witcher's "explanation," which has not been located, and Gilmer cautioned against punishing him if the Indians had been removed "as the object of punishment will have passed."[ccclxvii] Such was the political power of the local citizens during the removal crisis.

The story of Witcher's company is instructive as an indicator of the governor's lack of control over the local militia, the local popularity of rogue groups in the removal process, and the choices Cherokees were forced to make between flight, accommodation, and resistance. Witcher's behavior as organizer of an armed and unauthorized mob beyond the reach of discipline represents the worst expression of Georgia's callous behavior regarding the removal of Indians.

Military Occupation. In early April 1838, Asst. Adj. Gen. Mackay notified Quartermaster Hetzel that Capt. Wood would be mustered in and sent to Cedar Town.[ccclxviii] Wood, however, disappears from the records, and Witcher's company goes into service the next month, by request of the Cedar Town citizens (rather than the governor).[ccclxix] Apparently, neither Mackay nor Payne knew about Witcher because the May 11 order for the disposition of troops in Georgia authorized one (unnamed) company to take post at or near Cedar Town.[ccclxx] Two days later, Capt. Isaac S. Vincent of Clark County was mustered in for a three-month tour of duty with his company of 80 men.[ccclxxi] Gov. Gilmer had personally requested his service.[ccclxxii] Two days before the roundup was to begin, Vincent was ordered to Cedar Town.[ccclxxiii] Surprisingly, Vincent was never formally dismissed, and the year after the expulsion of Indians, he wrote to Col. Augustus Stokes requesting an official discharge. Stokes assumed Gen. Floyd mustered out all the Georgia troops.[ccclxxiv]

Construction. No construction has been identified for the Cedar Town encampment.

Supplies. Supplies for the encampment were assigned to Col. Cox at New Echota as early as mid-March.[ccclxxv] It will be useful to learn whether Witcher's company received supplies, but to this point, no records have been found regarding the receipt of forage or equipage in Cedar Town. On May 1, no corn or fodder was in storage, but 3,000 bushels of corn

and 10,000 bundles of fodder were obtainable.[ccclxxvi] Three weeks later, an invoice or ordinance stores showed that Vincent had received 81 muskets, 81 cartridge boxes, 81 cartridge box belts, 81 bayonet scabbards, 81 bayonet belts, and 81 bayonet belt plates.[ccclxxvii]

The ration records for Vincent's encampment are the most complete of any of the stations in Georgia. From them we learn that sick Indians, whether men, women, or children, were supposed to receive one-half pound of hard bread, and one pound of flour or three pints of corn for men, women, and children (an amount that could be enhanced if it proved insufficient). The ponies and horses of the prisoners were to be foraged, presumably on open fields.[ccclxxviii]

Isaac's provision returns for the prisoners "in his camp at Cedar Town" from May 28-June 26 show a total distribution of 2,986 bacon rations and 1,984 rations of hard bread. The bread was subsequently replaced by 326 rations of corn meal, which was itself replaced by 676 rations of flour.[ccclxxix] On June 17, plans to dispose of the public property were conveyed to Vincent, with instructions to provide six-to-eight days notice to the citizens for the auction held one day before the troops left the site. As usual, the presence of the quartermaster, Capt Cox, was deemed indispensable.[ccclxxx]

Prisoners. Vincent apparently captured the Cherokees in his assigned area promptly, but did not send them on to New Echota immediately. At the end of May, Scott ordered Vincent to send his Indian prisoners with their possessions and subsistence.[ccclxxxi] Two weeks later, Floyd wrote Vincent that he was glad the sick prisoners were convalescing and ordered him to canvass the area and seize any remaining Indians.[ccclxxxii] On June 21, Floyd again wrote Vincent and commanded him to return to New Echota with all his captives.[ccclxxxiii] Five days later, Vincent complied.

Vincent's provision returns indicate that he initially captured 153 Indians, a number that increased gradually over the next several days. Provisions were distributed to 153, then to 163, 166, and finally to 199 captives. On June 12, the number dropped sharply to 18 Indians, presumably those too sick to travel, and that number remained stable until June 26.[ccclxxxiv]

Camp Scott (Rome, Floyd County)

Information about Camp Scott at Rome is incomplete and does not offer clues to the specific location of the post. Useful resources are relatively evenly divided between the letter book of Gen. Wool, the governor's correspondence at the Georgia Department of Archives and History, and the microfilm records of the Cherokee removal housed at the National Archives Records Administration in East Point, Georgia. However, because the camp was occupied more than once, hope remains that considerably more information can be found. Georgia chapter member Doug Mabry has been researching deeds at the Floyd County courthouse with the hope of finding land transfers that include information about Camp Scott, and he remains optimistic that he can locate the site.

Sometime before 1836, Camp Scott (doubtless named for Gen. Winfield Scott, who was serving in the Seminole War in 1836) was established in Rome, Georgia, in the Etowah District of the Cherokee Nation. Several factors made Rome an important place to the military. Located at the confluence of three rivers -- the Coosa, the Etowah, and the Oostanaula -- Rome was geographically close to the Creek as well as the Cherokee Nations, and was the community

where John Ross, John Ridge, and Major Ridge all had plantations and ferries. Rome also stood at the intersection of the north-south Alabama Road (that led to the Federal Road) and the east-west Alabama Road (that led across the southern part of the Cherokee Nation to Alabama). Finally, Rome was the main river port between Gadsden, Alabama and Calhoun, Georgia. Founded in 1834, Rome became the county seat for Floyd County, which was established in 1832.

John Ross

The homes and properties of the wealthiest men in the Cherokee Nation became available to the Georgians following the 1832 Cherokee lottery. In the Rome area, such homeowners included Ross, the two Ridges, and several members of the Vann family. Since the Ridges were leaders of the so-called Treaty Party, their property was given a measure of protection until after they departed from Georgia. John Ross was not as fortunate.

In mid-March, 1835, William N. Bishop authorized one Stephen Carter to take over the lot where Ross had made his home. Situated at the head of the Coosa River, the two-story house with four fireplaces and a veranda that spanned the length of one side of the house was valued at more than 3 thousand dollars. The lot included at least 16 additional buildings such as a kitchen, slave quarters, stables, corncribs, a blacksmith shop, and a smokehouse. [ccclxxxv] By the fall of 1835, the dispossessed Ross had moved into the Cherokee Nation in Tennessee. Although his Georgia home site has been developed, a Trail of Tears marker could be placed in the vicinity to identify Ross's role in leading a brilliant protest against removal to the west.

Like Spring Place, Camp Scott had early ties to the Georgia militia. In 1836, anxiety about the Creeks who had been expelled from Georgia in 1826, led the governor to place 200 men at the head of Coosa River under the command of then-Major Charles H. Nelson of the Georgia Guard and the Highland Mounted Battalion.[ccclxxxvi] Nelson had previously participated (or led) the arrest and confinement of the missionaries at Spring Place. The battalion remained until late September, and then mustered out.[ccclxxxvii] By the fall of 1836, the post was called Camp Scott.

A review of the compensation claims submitted in 1842 by Cherokees indicated that the phrase "head of Coosa" commonly referred to a residential community. *Te ses ke, Nah che yah, Kah too wa lah ta*, Noisy Water, Celia, and Leaf Bow, for example, all claimed property left at their homes at the head of Coosa.[ccclxxxviii]

Military Occupation. Stationed in Rome by the governor, Nelson and his troops fell under the command of Gen. John E. Wool in late July 1836. Wool's confidence in Nelson was demonstrated by the orders given for Nelson to examine the militia command in Cherokee County, Georgia and Cherokee County, Alabama, to investigate the seizure of Major Ridge's ferry in Rome, and to proceed with the capture of refugee or escaped Creeks.[ccclxxxix] Before his term of service expired in the fall, Nelson was authorized to investigate the possible seizure of John Ridge's ferry.[cccxc] No members of Nelson's troops have been identified other than Lt. Elias Henderson, the quartermaster at Camp Scott.[cccxci] In September, 1836, Gen. Wool ordered Maj. M. M. Payne to Camp Scott to muster out Nelson and his regiment, and to await Capt. McClellan who was escorting Creeks to Gunter's Landing.[cccxcii]

Three other Rome volunteer companies were organized by the time of Cherokee removal, but none seems to have been stationed in Rome. Samuel Stewart, commanding Colonel of a regiment raised in 1837, was responsible for investigating rumors of Indian hostilities, but apparently was not otherwise involved in the removal process.[cccxciii]

In May 1838, John T. Story (also spelled Storey) and Edward Stuart, both of Rome, reported that they had raised a regiment to assist with Cherokee removal and offered their services to Gen. Scott.[cccxciv] Six days later, the order for the distribution of militia companies placed Story in Rome along with Capt. (Charles H.?) Campbell, but no mention is found of Stuart.[cccxcv] More than 150 men camped at Scott during its second occupation, and on June 9, Floyd ordered them to return to New Echota for mustering out.[cccxcvi]

Construction. Although Camp Scott was never identified as a fort, and, presumably, never had a stockade or barracks, some kind of construction would have been necessary to store the arms and supplies kept at the post. The 1836 occupation entailed weapons, munitions, forage, horses, and rations, all of which would require storage facilities. Although it is possible the troops rented stables in Rome, no rental invoices have been located. If the facilities remained intact, the second occupation may not have necessitated additional construction.

Supplies. In 1836, the state sent arms, ammunition, and supplies to Cherokee County, with instructions to Gen. Hemphill in Rome to send for them.[cccxcvii] In addition to munitions, the post apparently had wagons and teams for the fall transport of Creek prisoners.[cccxcviii] When Nelson mustered out, he left 100 stands of muskets, as well as cartridge boxes, bayonets, and scabbards.[cccxcix] The state arms and ammunition were ordered sent to the Augusta Arsenal, and Wool took charge of the materials belonging to the federal government. Interestingly, Wool had no funds to pay for the supplies of the company and as a result, Nelson paid for them, on credit, for a period of three months.[cd]

Nearly two years later, an inventory of goods turned over by Nelson and left at Raymond Sanford's home in Hall County included 120 stands of arms, two horses, six pounds of iron, medicines, muskets, tents, and camp kettles.[cdi] In addition, Robert Ware of Rome reported that Nelson left at Camp Scott, "near my residence," 100 stands of muskets, and cartridge boxes, bayonets, and scabbards.[cdii] The state's indifference to the collection of its own supplies, particularly stock and weapons, underscores the complexity it faced in the removal of Indians.

Although it is unclear when Camp Scott was reoccupied, in early April 1838, Hetzel sent bills for the transport of camp and garrison equipage and subsistence stores to Rome, presumably Camp Scott.[cdiii] All troops mustered in at New Echota received ordinance supplies there, and sometime around May 23, Story and Campbell received muskets, cartridge boxes, cartridge box belts, scabbards, bayonet belts, belt plates, screw drivers, wipers, ball screws, spring vices, musket ball cartridges, flints, and gun slings for more than 75 men each.[cdiv] By mid-June, plans were under way for the sale of all public property that remained at Camp Scott. As he did for several other posts, Col Cox planned to supervise the auction.[cdv]

Prisoners. In the fall of 1836, Capt. McClellan escorted an unknown number of Creek prisoners from Camp Scott to Gunter's Landing.[cdvi] In late May, 1838, Capt. Campbell reported that the company at Rome had captured 70 Indians, and by June 9, Floyd told Scott that all Indians had been removed from the neighborhood of Rome.[cdvii] The records do not clarify questions about the route taken by the prisoners, nor their final destination. They may have taken the east-west Alabama road to Ft. Payne, Alabama. Alternatively, they may have gone north to Ft. Cumming and from there on to Ross's Landing.

Perkins, Dade County

Research in the National Archives in Washington resulted in the recognition that an authentic effort was made to establish a post near Perkins' in Dade County. One reference to such a camp was found in the collected materials relating to Cherokee removal found on microfilm at the National Archives Records Administration in East Point, Georgia. The only additional references to the Dade County camp are found in the quartermaster's records that indicate that preparations were made for the camp, and one man was sent to set it up. The initiative was undertaken after most of the Indians had been removed from the state and, as it turned out, no camp was ever set up and no company was ever sent.

Dade County lies on the Appalachian Plateau in the extreme northwest corner of the state and, at the time of removal, was inaccessible from Georgia because Lookout and Sand Mountains created an impassable barrier between Dade and the adjacent counties. Lookout Valley, watered by Lookout Creek, lies between the two mountains and provided homes to the Cherokees. At the time of removal, the county could be entered only from Tennessee or Alabama.

Although no information was found to identify Perkins, Dade County genealogist Sue Forrester graciously agreed to research the Perkins name in the county records. She found that one Isham Perkins sold land on both sides of Lookout Creek in 1842, but records of his original purchase or winning of the lot are missing. In 1848, Perkins sold another lot, also on both sides of Lookout Creek, to James Catchersides. That same year, Perkins initiated a sale that was not completed until 1853, after his death. No records were found of Perkins as a storeowner, Indian agent, or tavern keeper, any of which would have made him a familiar figure to the military in Tennessee. Research will continue.

Military Occupation. The establishment of a post in Dade County was anticipated by May 14 when the order was made for the disposition of troops in Alabama, Georgia, and Tennessee. The order called for one Alabama Company to take post near Perkins' in Dade County.[cdviii] The order thus placed the camp in the western military district, beyond the command of Gen. Floyd at New Echota. Approximately two weeks later, Capt. C. H. Goldsborough, who was an agent of the Indian department, was ordered to take charge of supplies at Perkins'.[cdix] The following day, Goldsborough was named quartermaster for the anticipated post.[cdx]

In early June, Goldsborough reported that he had selected a good spot for the camp about ¾ miles southeast of Perkins,' a site that might fail to meet the approval of the "Alabama captain."[cdxi] Apparently Goldsborough had already unfavorably encountered his commander. On June 9, Hetzel received notice that Col. Lindsay had abandoned plans for a camp at Perkins', and two days later ordered Goldsborough to Ft. Cass for other duties.[cdxii]

Supplies. Apparently, the post's supplies were sent to Dade County ahead of the quartermaster, a sure indication that Perkins was

well known to the military. When Goldsborough was ordered to the post, he was told to "take charge of the stores now at that post and make the necessary arrangement to store them."[cdxiii] The directive lends credence to the notion that Perkins was a storeowner, or at least owned considerable storage facilities. That same day, by separate letter, Goldsborough was told to rent buildings if possible since the quartermaster department would not need storehouses in Dade County for long.[cdxiv]

Goldsborough was concerned about supplying the still-unidentified company. Not knowing what to do if the troops arrived without tents and camp equipage, he was particularly worried about purchasing tents since he thought he could acquire camp equipage at Ross's Landing.[cdxv] The fact that an employee of the Indian department would be sent to a station without information about how to execute their orders indicates the surprisingly unorganized nature of the removal process. Although Hetzel wrote a memo that he had contacted a Dr. Harris to supply the post with necessary equipment, no such letter was found.[cdxvi]

Perhaps the most surprising data about the Dade County post is that Goldsborough never built or obtained a storehouse for the company provisions. He remarked that he was unable to complete a storehouse and the provisions had been left in a very "contracted building" that was so small he could not even take an inventory of the goods.[cdxvii] His final order regarding the supplies was to turn them over to the quartermaster at Ft. Payne, Alabama.[cdxviii]

Prisoners. Regardless of the apparent lack or organization at the purported camp, 60 Indians were collected in Dade County and sent to Ross's Landing. Certainly Goldsborough did not capture them since he did not have a company. On June 2, Lindsay reported to Gen. Scott that the county was bereft of Indians, apparently due to the efforts of Maj. Dulaney.[cdxix]

[i] Thomas W. Hodler and Howard R. Schretter, <u>The Atlas of Georgia</u> (Athens, GA: The Institute of Community and Area Development, 1986), 16-17.
[ii] Thomas W. Hodler and Howard R. Schretter, <u>The Atlas of Georgia</u> (Athens, GA: The Institute of Community and Area Development, 1986), 16-17.
[iii] Hodler and Schretter, <u>Georgia Atlas</u>, p. 17.
[iv] Hodler and Schretter, <u>Georgia Atlas</u>, 16-17.
[v] Thomas W. Hodler and Howard R. Schretter, <u>The Atlas of Georgia</u> (Athens, GA: The Institute of Community and Area Development, 1986), 16-17.
[vi] <u>Georgia: The WPA Guide to its Towns and Countryside</u> (Columbia, SC: University of South Carolina Press, 1940), 400, 477.
[vii] Michael A. Godfrey, <u>A Sierra Club Naturalist's Guide to the Piedmont</u> (San Francisco: Sierra Club Books, 1980), 10-15.
[viii] <u>Georgia: The WPA Guide to its Towns and Countryside</u> (Columbia, SC: University of South Carolina Press, 1940), 9.
[ix] Hodler and Schretter, <u>Georgia Atlas</u>, 17.
[x] Anonymous, "Cherokee History, Habits, Language," Ayer Collection, Newberry Library, Chicago, np.
[xi] Sarah H. Hill, <u>Weaving New Worlds: Southeastern Cherokee Women and Their Basketry</u> (Chapel Hill: University of North Carolina Press, 1997), 10. These uses were commented on by European travelers in the late 1700s.
[xii] Hodler and Schretter, <u>Georgia Atlas</u>, 54.
[xiii] Gayther L. Plummer, "18th Century Forests in Georgia," <u>Bulletin of the Georgia Academy of Sciences</u> 33 (1975): 8.
[xiv] Michael A. Godfrey, <u>A Sierra Club Naturalist's Guide to the Piedmont</u> (San Francisco: Sierra Club Books, 1980), 137-38.
[xv] Hodler and Schretter, <u>Georgia Atlas</u>, 52.
[xvi] Plummer, "18th Century Forests," 16.
[xvii] Godfrey, <u>Sierra Club Naturalist's Guide</u>, 137.
[xviii] Michael A. Godfrey, <u>Sierra Club Naturalist's Guide,</u> 200.
[xix] Hodler and Schretter, <u>Georgia Atlas</u>, 52.
[xx] Ann Sutton and Myron Sutton, <u>Eastern Forests</u> (New York: Alfred A. Knopf, 1985), 59.
[xxi] <u>WPA Guide to Georgia</u>, 20-21.
[xxii] Godfrey, <u>Sierra Club Naturalist's Guide</u>, 142-43
[xxiii] Hodler and Schretter, <u>Georgia Atlas</u>, 39.
[xxiv] Hodler and Schretter, <u>Georgia Atlas</u>, 41.
[xxv] Godfrey, <u>Sierra Club Naturalist's Guide</u>, 35.
[xxvi] Hodler and Schretter, <u>Georgia Atlas</u>, 37.
[xxvii] Godfrey, <u>Sierra Club Naturalist's Guide</u>, 34.
[xxviii] Wilms, "Cherokee Land Use," 23.
[xxix] John Ridge, "Letter to Albert Gallatin, February 27, 1826," in Theda Perdue and Michael D. Green, <u>The Cherokee removal, A Brief History with</u>

Documents (Boston: Bedford Books of St. Martin's press, 1995), 35.
[xxx] Wilms, "Cherokee Land Use," 18.
[xxxi] Wilms, "Cherokee Land Use," 23.
[xxxii] Ridge, "Letter to Albert Gallatin," 35.
[xxxiii] Wilms, "Cherokee Land Use," 16-17.
[xxxiv] "Articles of Agreement between the United States and the Cherokee Nation for opening a road from the State of Tennessee to the State of Georgia through the Cherokee Nation (recorded by Return J. Meigs), Oct. 20, 1803." http://neptune3.galib.uga.edu, 24 July, 2004. William McLoughlin notes that the effort to construct such a road had begun in 1799 in the administration of John Adams: McLoughlin, <u>Cherokee Renascence in the New Republic</u> (Princeton: Princeton University Press, 1986), 77.
[xxxv] Charles C. Royce, <u>Cherokee Nation of Indians</u> (Chicago: Aldine Publishing, 1975), 59.
[xxxvi] Articles of Agreement between the United States and the Cherokee Nation for opening a road from the state of Tennessee to the state of Georgia through the Cherokee Nation [recorded by Return J. Meigs]" Oct. 20, 1803. <u>Southeastern Native American Documents 1730-1842</u> http://neptune3.galib.uga.edu 24 July 2004.
[xxxvii] "Articles of Agreement between the United States and the Cherokee Nation for opening a road from the state of Tennessee to the state of Georgia through the Cherokee Nation [recorded by Return J. Meigs]" Oct. 20, 1803. <u>Southeastern Native American Documents 1730-1842</u> http://neptune3.galib.uga.edu 24 July 2004.
[xxxviii] Clemens de Baillou, <u>Early Georgia</u> 2(2), 1957:10.
[xxxix] "Letter 1804 July 6, Athens, Georgia [to] John Sevier, Governor, Knoxville, Tennessee/W Barnett, B Harris," <u>Southeastern Native American Documents, 1730-1842.</u> http://neptune3.galib.uga.edu 24 July, 2004.
[xl] "Letter 1804 July 19, Knoxville, Tennessee [to] Colo William Barnett and Brigadier general B Harris, Jackson County, Georgia/John Sevier," and "Letter 1804 Aug. 9, Knoxville, Tennessee to Col. Joseph McMin, Colo Samuel Wear, and Maj John Cowan/John Sevier," <u>Southeastern Native American Documents, 1730-1842.</u> http://neptune3.galib.uga.edu 24 July, 2004.
[xli] James L. Douthat, comp., <u>Colonel Return Jonathan Meigs Day Book Number 2</u> (Signal Mountain, Tn: Institute of Historical Research, 1993), 41, 56, 62.
[xlii] James L. Douthat, comp., <u>Colonel Return Jonathan Meigs Day Book Number 2</u> (Signal Mountain, Tn: Institute of Historical Research, 1993), pp. 32, 37, 42, 59, 67, 84, 89.
[xliii] In their diaries of a journey to the Cherokee nation in 1800 Moravian missionaries Abraham Steiner and Frederich de Schweinitz wrote that James Vann's home "lies on the trail between South Carolina and Georgia…too near the road" where a mission would be disturbed by the high number of traveling Indians: Edmund D. Schwartz, <u>History of the Moravian Missions Among Southern Indian Tribes of the United States</u> (Bethlehem, PA: Times Publishing Co., 1923),

56-7. When the Federal Road was built it passed by the Vann home.

[xliv] Don L. Shadburn, Cherokee Planters in Georgia 1832-1838 (Roswell, GA: WH Wolfe Associates, 1990), 72.

[xlv] Gary E Moulton, ed., The Papers of Chief John Ross 1 (Norman, Ok: University of Oklahoma Press, 1985), 109.

[xlvi] Marion Hemperley, Retracing the Old Federal Road," A North Geeorgia Journal of History 1(1989):265.

[xlvii] "Acts of the General Assembly of the State of Georgia, Passed in November and December, 1842. Incorporations, 109. http://neptune3.galib.uga.edu 24 July, 2004.

[xlviii] "Newton's Visit," 112.

[xlix] "Ebenezer Newton Visits the Cherokees," in Edward J. Cashin, ed., A Wilderness Still the Cradle of Nature (Savannah, GA: The Beehive Press, 1994), 112.

[l] Don L. Shadburn, Unhallowed Intrusion: A History of Cherokee Families in Forsyth County, Georgia (Saline, MI: McNaughton and Gunn, 1993), 534-37, 687.

[li] Robert S. Davis, Jr., "The Indians of Pickens County," A North Georgia Journal of History 3 (1986): 319.

[lii] Charles J. Kappler, comp. and ed., Indian Treaties 1778-1883 (Mattituck, NY: Amereon House, 1972), 83-4.

[liii] Wilson Lumpkin, The Removal of the Cherokee Indians from Georgia 1 (Savannah, GA: The Savannah Morning News Print, 1907), 300.

[liv] Matt Gedney, Living on the Unicoi Road (Marietta, GA: Little Star press, 1996), 19-20.

[lv] Don L. Shadburn, Cherokee Planters in Georgia 1832-1838 (Roswell, GA: WH Wolfe Associates, 1990), 14.

[lvi] Marion Hemperley, "The Alabama Roads," A North Georgia Journal of History 2, 1 (1991):

[lvii] Marion Hemperley, "The Alabama Roads," A North Georgia Journal of History 2, 1 (1991):

[lviii] Marion Hemperley, "The Alabama Roads," A North Georgia Journal of History 2, 1 (1991):

[lix] In Don L. Shadburn, Cherokee Planters in Georgia 1832-1838 (Roswell, GA: WH Wolfe Associates, 1990), 12.

[lx] Marion Hemperley, "The Alabama Roads," A North Georgia Journal of History 2, 1 (1991):

[lxi] Georgia Trail of Tears member Bob Faye, personal communication.

[lxii] In Don L. Shadburn, Cherokee Planters in Georgia 1832-1838 (Roswell, GA: WH Wolfe Associates, 1990), 26n.

[lxiii] NARA RG 393 M1475 R2 fr0489.

[lxiv] Marion Hemperley, "The Alabama Roads," A North Georgia Journal of History 2, 1 (1991):

[lxv] NARA RG 393 M11475 r2, fr 0488-90.

[lxvi] "The Journal of Rev. Daniel S. Butrick, May 19-1838-April 1, 1839," Cherokee Removal Monograph One (Park Hill, Ok: The Trail of Tears Association Oklahoma Chapter, 1998), 2,3.

[lxvii] "Acts of the General Assembly of the State of Georgia, Passed in Milledgeville at an Annual Session in November and December, 1834. Roads and Canals," 209. http://neptune3.galib.uga.edu 24 July, 2004.

[lxviii] "Acts of the General Assembly of the State of Georgia, Passed in Milledgeville at an Annual Session in November and December, 1836. Roads," 243. http://neptune3.galib.uga.edu 24 July, 2004.

[lxix] "Acts of the General Assembly of the State of Georgia, Passed in Milledgeville at an Annual Session in November and December, 1837," 241. http://neptune3.galib.uga.edu 24 July, 2004

[lxx] "Acts of the General Assembly of the State of Georgia, Passed in Milledgeville at an Annual Session in November and December, 1808," 37. http://neptune3.galib.uga.edu 24 July, 2004.

[lxxi] "Acts of the General Assembly of the State of Georgia, Passed in Milledgeville at an Annual Session in November and December, 1836," 249. http://neptune3.galib.uga.edu 31 July, 2004

[lxxii] NARA RG 393 M1474 R2 fr0489.

[lxxiii] "Acts of the General Assembly of the State of Georgia, Passed in Milledgeville at an Annual Session in November and December, 1834," 204. http://neptune3.galib.uga.edu 31 July, 2004

[lxxiv] "Acts of the General Assembly of the State of Georgia, Passed in Milledgeville at an Annual Session in November and December, 1836," 247. http://neptune3.galib.uga.edu 31 July, 2004

[lxxv] Draft Version, An Act to Appropriate money for the support of Government…1836," 28. http://…legis-idx.pl?sessionid28 December, 2000.

[lxxvi] "Acts of the General Assembly of the State of Georgia, Passed in Milledgeville at an Annual Session in November and December, 1837," 244, 246. http://neptune3.galib.uga.edu 24 July, 2004

[lxxvii] NARA RG 393 M1475 R2 fr 0489.

[lxxviii] NARA RG 393 M14475 R1 fr 0161.

[lxxix] NA RG 92 Entry 352 Box 3.

[lxxx] Wilson Lumpkin, Removal of the Cherokees, 1, 353-56.

[lxxxi] Wilson Lumpkin, Removal of the Cherokees 2, 10.

[lxxxii] Gen. John Wool to Capt. Vernon, July 23, 1836, Box 52, File 19, Letterbook July 1836-April 1837, John Ellis Wool Papers, New York State Library, Albany.

[lxxxiii] Gen. John Wool to Lt. Howe, July 25, 1836, Box 52, File 19, Letterbook July 1836-April 1837, John Ellis Wool Papers, New York State Library, Albany.

[lxxxiv] Wilson Lumpkin, Removal of the Cherokees 2, 8.

lxxxv Wilson Lumpkin, Removal of the Cherokees 2, 40.

lxxxvi "No. 26 Coltharp and McSpadden 10 Dec. 1836," John Ellis Wool Papers Box 25 Folders 5-6, New York State Library, Albany.

lxxxvii Coltharp and McSpadden 10 Dec. 1836," John Ellis Wool Papers Box 25 Folders 5-6, New York State Library, Albany.

lxxxviii See for example Gen. Wool to Lumpkin and Kennedy, March 2, 1837, Box 52, File 19, Letterbook July 1836-April 1837, John Ellis Wool Papers, New York State Library, Albany.

lxxxix Thos. Lyon, Ft. Cass, to Lt. Hoskins Papers of John Ellis Wool, Box 52, File 19, Letter book July 1836-April 1837, New York State Library, Albany, 177.

xc Gen. Wool, New Echota, to Capt. Samuel N. Barnes, Nov. 19, 1836, Ibid, 194-95; Thos. Lyon, New Echota, to Capt. E. Buffington, Dec. 10, 1836, Papers of John Ellis Wool, Box 52, File 19, Letter book July 1836-April 1837, New York State Library, Albany, 213. Each company was to have "50 privates, officers, non commissioned officers, and musicians, and each non com officer, musician, and private must have a good horse, saddle, bridle, martingale and blanket and himself well clothed including an overcoat and blanket and at least one spur. Each officer will be armed with a sword and if practicable with pistols:" Papers of John Ellis Wool, Box 52, File 19, Letter book July 1836-April 1837, New York State Library, Albany, 181.

xci NA RG 93 Entry 350 box 2 vol 1 145-48.

xcii Wilson Lumpkin, Removal of the Cherokees 2, 92-3.

xciii Gen. Wool, New Echota, to Lt. Howe, Jan. 24, 1837, Box 52, File 19, Letterbook July 1836-April 1837, John Ellis Wool Papers, New York State Library, Albany, 254.

xciv Dec. 9, 1836: Thos. Lyon, New Echota, to Cap. Derrick Box 52, File 19, Letterbook July 1836-April 1837, John Ellis Wool Papers, New York State Library, Albany, 211.

xcv Gen. Wool, New Echota, to Gen. R. Jones, Feb. 18, 1838, Box 52, File 19, Letterbook July 1836-April 1837, John Ellis Wool Papers, New York State Library, Albany, 289-90.

xcvi Wilson Lumpkin, Removal of the Cherokees 2, 144-45.

xcvii March 1, 1838, Col. Lindsay, New Echota, to Gov. Gilmer, Georgia Dept of Archives and History, RG 1-1-5, Drawer 223, Letters and Orders of Gov. Gilmer Relating to the Removal of Indians.

xcviii Feb. 25, 1838, A. Cox, New Echota, to Lt. A.R.Hetzel, National Archives RG 92 Entry 352 Box 3.

xcix NARA RG 393 m1475 r1, fr 0500-01.

c Feb. 25, 1838, A. Cox, New Echota, to Lt. A.R.Hetzel, National Archives RG 92 Entry 352 Box 3.

ci NA RG 92 Entry 352 Box 3.

cii NA RG 92 Entry 352 Box 3.

ciii NA RG 92 Entry 357, Box 6.

civ NA RG 92 Entry 352 Box 3.

cv NARA RG 393 m1475 r1 fr 0285.

cvi NARA RG 393 m1475 r1 fr 0403-05.

cvii GDAH Gov Gilmer Correspondence RG 1-1-5 Box 19, 335.

cviii NARA RG 393 m1475 r1 fr 0663-64.

cix NARA RG 393 m1475 r1 fr 0847-50, 0953-54.

cx Marybelle Chase, 1842 Claims Skin Bayou District, 210.

cxi Cherokee Advance July 4, 1890, p. 3, col. 2.

cxii Cherokee Advance, July 4, 1890, p. 3, col. 1.

cxiii Cherokee County Land Records, Book 1, 296-97.

cxiv Cherokee Advance Friday Feb. 4, 1888, p. 3 col. 2. I am grateful to John Carver of Canton for providing me with a copy of the article for this report.

cxv See Cherokee Advance April 24, 1903, p. 3 column 6.

cxvi Thos. Lyon, New Echota, to Capt. E Buffington, Dec. 10, 1836, Box 52, File 19, Letterbook July 1836-April 1837, John Ellis Wool Papers, New York State Library, Albany, 213-14.

cxvii NARA RG 393 m1475 r1 fr 0239-42.

cxviii NARA RG 393 m1475 r1 fr 0627.

cxix NARA RG 393 m1475 r1 fr 0628-29.

cxx NARA RG 393 m1475 r2 fr 0529.

cxxi NARA RG 393 m1475 r2 fr 0529.

cxxii NA RG 92 Entry 357 Box 6.

cxxiii NA RG 92 Entry 352 Letters received

cxxiv GDAH RG 1-1-5 Letters and Orders of Gov. George Gilmer Relating to the Removal of Indians (also on microfilm, drawer 223)

cxxv NA RG 92 Entry 350 Box 2 Vol. 2 Letterbook pp. 150, 158.

cxxvi See, for example, Capt. Hitchcock of Walker County, April 2, 1838, GDAH RG 1-1-5, Box 19, Letters and Orders of Gov. George Gilmer Relating to the Removal of Indians.

cxxvii NA RG 393 m1475 r1 fr 0405. 0533.

cxxviii NA RG 393 m1475 r1 fr 0500-01.

cxxix See, for example, the 1834 H. S. Tanner map of the United States of America, the 1846 S. Augustus Mitchell map of Georgia, and the 1863 A.J. Johnson map of Georgia and Alabama on which the name is recorded as Sutalle.

cxxx R. Jerald Ledbetter, W. Dean Wood, Karen G. Wood, Robbie F. Etheridge, and Chad O. Braley, Cultural Resources Survey of Allatoona Lake Area Georgia Vol. 1 (Athens, GA: Southeast Archaeological Services, 1987), typescript, pp. 287-92.

cxxxi GDAH, Letters Talks Treaties, 489. Brewster is later found living in Etowah, which was renamed Canton.

cxxxii David Williams, The Georgia Gold Rush, Twenty-Niners, Cherokees, and Gold fever (Columbia, SC: University of South Carolina Press, 1993), 25-6.

[cxxxiii] Lt. Abram C. Fowler to Maj. Wager, Sept. 26, 1830, in Williams, Georgia Gold Rush, 33.

[cxxxiv] GDAH, Letters Talks Treaties, 489.

[cxxxv] George White, Historical Collections of Georgia (New York: Pudney and Russell, 1854), 390.

[cxxxvi] Minutes of the Cherokee County Inferior Court, April 13, 1835, 31.

[cxxxvii] Shadburn, Cherokee Planters in Georgia, 62.

[cxxxviii] NARA RG 303 m1475 r1 fr 0209-10.

[cxxxix] NARA RG 393 m1475 r1 fr 0351-53.

[cxl] GDAH RG 2-4-46 Box 75 Folder 11.

[cxli] NARA RG 393 m1475 r1 fr 0272-77.

[cxlii] NARA RG 393 m1475 r1 fr 0351-53.

[cxliii] NARA RG 92 Entry 350 Box 2 Vol 2 303-04.

[cxliv] NARA RG 393 m1475 r1 fr 0637-39.

[cxlv] GDAH Cherokee Letters Talks Treaties, 247.

[cxlvi] NARA RG 393 m1475 r1 fr 0500-01.

[cxlvii] NARA RG 393 m1475 r1 fr 0554-56.

[cxlviii] NARA RG 393 m1475 r1 fr 0272-77.

[cxlix] Andrew W. Cain, History of Lumpkin County for the First Hundred years 1832-1932 (Atlanta: Stein Printing Co., 1932), 127.

[cl] David Williams, The Georgia Gold Rush (Columbia, SC: University of South Carolina Press, 1993), 62.

[cli] Sylvia Head and Elizabeth Etheridge, The Neighborhood Mint (Alpharetta, GA: Gold Rush Gallery, 2000), 5.

[clii] Ibid, 18-19.

[cliii] Ibid, 35-44.

[cliv] Don L. Shadburn, Cherokee Planters in Georgia, 1832-1838 (Roswell, GA: W.H. Wolfe Associates, 1990), 227.

[clv] Ibid, 230-31.

[clvi] GDAH Letters and Orders of Gov. Gilmer 1837-1838.

[clvii] Ibid.

[clviii] Ibid, NA RG 92 Entry 350 Box 2 Vol. 2, 171-72.

[clix] NA RG 92 Entry 352 Box 3.

[clx] GDAH Cherokee Letters Talks Treaties vol. 3, 699.

[clxi] NA RG 92 Entry 352 Box 6, Entry 357 Box 6.

[clxii] NA RG 92 Entry 352 Box 3.

[clxiii] GDAH, Letters and Orders of Gov. Gilmer, 1837-1838.

[clxiv] http://rootsweb.com/pub/usgenweb/ga/military/Indian, 28 Sept. 2004.;

[clxv] NA RG 92 Entry 352 Box 3, Entry 357 Box 6.

[clxvi] GDAH, RG 1-1-5, Letters and Orders of Gov. George Gilmer Relating to the Removal of Indians (also on microfilm, drawer 223); GDAH Cherokee Letters talks Treaties vol. 3.

[clxvii] March 25, 1838, A.R. Hetzel to Benj. Cleveland, NA RG 92 Entry 350 Box 2 Vol. 2, 225.

[clxviii] Cain, History of Lumpkin County, 127.

[clxix] GDAH RG 1-1-5 Box 19 Letters and Orders of Gov. George Gilmer Relating to the Removal of Indians (also on microfilm, drawer 223).

[clxx] NA RG 92 Entry 352 Box 3; ibid Box 2, Vol. 2.

[clxxi] NARA RG 393 m1475 r1 fr 0401-03.

[clxxii] George Gordon Ward, The Annals of Upper Georgia centered in Gilmer County (Nashville: The Parthenon Press, 1965), 56.

[clxxiii] Shadburn, Cherokee Planters in Georgia,, 189-92.

[clxxiv] NA RG 92 Entry 357 Box 6.

[clxxv] NA RG 92 Entry 350 Box 2.

[clxxvi] NA RG 92 Entry 352 Box 3.

[clxxvii] NA RG 92 Entry 350 Box 2 Vol. 2 214; NARA RG 393 m1475 r1 fr0256-57.

[clxxviii] GDAH RG 1-1-5 Box 19.

[clxxix] NARA RG 393 m1475 r1 fr 0749-51.

[clxxx] NARA RG 393 m1475 r1 fr 1037-38.

[clxxxi] NA RG 92 Entry 357 Box 6.

[clxxxii] NA RG 92 entry 352 Box 3.

[clxxxiii] NA RG 92 Entry 350 Box 2 Vol. 2, 152, 153, 157.

[clxxxiv] NA RG 92 Entry 352 Box 6; see also RG 92 Entry 225 Box 304 Folder Cherokee Indians 1879.

[clxxxv] NA RG 92 Entry 350 Box 2 Vol. 2 195, 199; NA RG 352 Box 3.

[clxxxvi] NA RG 92 Entry 352 Box 3.

[clxxxvii] NARA RG 393 m1475 r1 fr 0965-68; NARA RG 393 m1475 r1 fr0539.

[clxxxviii] NARA RG 393 m1475 r1 fr 0536-37.

[clxxxix] NARA RG 393 m1475 r1 fr 0408-10.

[cxc] NARA RG 393 m1475 r1 fr 0539.

[cxci] NARA RG 393 m1475 r1 fr 0752-54.

[cxcii] Gardner, Cherokees and Baptists, 104

[cxciii] Gardner, Cherokees and Baptists, 137-38.

[cxciv] Gardner, Cherokees and Baptists, 104-06.

[cxcv] Gardner, Cherokees and Baptists, 185-90.

[cxcvi] Shadburn, Cherokee Planters, 241-45.

[cxcvii] July 23, 1836, Gen. Wool to J.A. Bell, Letterbook, 42-4.

[cxcviii] Vivki Rozema, Footsteps of the Cherokees (Winston-Salem, NC: John F. Blair, 1995), 323.

[cxcix] www.greatlakesofgeorgia.com 11 October, 2004.

[cc] March 23, 1837, Gen. Wool , New Echota, to Capt. Derrick, Wool Letterbook, 332-33..

[cci] March 25, 1837, Gen. Wool, New Echota, to Capt. Derrick, Wool Lettebook, 339.

[ccii] GDAH Cherokee Letters Talks Treaties, Vol. 3, 701.

[cciii] NA RG 92 Entry 352 Box 3; ibid.

[cciv] NARA RG 393 m1475 r1 fr 0363.

[ccv] Georgia Military Affairs 1838-1842, typescript, WPA Project 5993 directed by Mrs. J. E. Hays, 1940.

[ccvi] NARA RG 393 m1475 r1 fr 0405; ibid, fr 0430-31.

[ccvii] NARA RG 393 m1475 r1 fr 0860-62..

[ccviii] NARA RG 393 m1475 r1 fr 0500-01.

[ccix] NA RG 92 Entry 352 Box 6, Entry 357 Box 6.

[ccx] NA RG 92 Entry 352 Box 3.

[ccxi] NA RG 92 Entry 350 Box 2, Vol. 2.

[ccxii] NA RG 92 Entry 350 Box 2 Vol. 2 232.

[ccxiii] NA RG 92 Entry 350 Box 2 Vol. 2 260; NA RG 92 Entry 352 Box 3.

[ccxiv] NARA RG 393 m1475 r1 p. 137.

[ccxv] NA RG 92 Entry 352 Box 3.

[ccxvi] NA RG 92 Entry 352 Box 3.

[ccxvii] NARA RG 393 m1475 r1 fr 0930-32.

[ccxviii] NA RG 92 Entry 352, Box 3.

[ccxix] NA RG 92 Entry 352 Box 3.

[ccxx] NARA RG 393 m1475 r1 fr 0433-34.

[ccxxi] NARA RG 393 m1475 r1 fr 0577-83.

[ccxxii] Feb. 18, 1840, Ben Poore, Coosawattee, to Gorham Parsons, http://neptune3.galib.uga.edu 12 October, 2004.

[ccxxiii] Charles O. Walker, Cherokee Footprints Vol. 2 (Canton, GA: Industrial Printing, 1989), 18.

[ccxxiv] Shadburn, Cherokee Planters, 196-97. Two of George's slaves, Daniel and Nanny, had converted to Christianity, probably by Baptist missionary Elisha Battle: see Robert G. Gardner, Cherokees and Baptists in Georgia (Atlanta: Georgia Baptist Historical Society, 1989), 64 n. 11.

[ccxxv] Walker, Cherokee Footprints Vol. 1, 133.

[ccxxvi] Robert G. Gardner, Cherokees and Baptists in Georgia (Atlanta: Georgia Baptist Historical Society, 1989), 136-37.

[ccxxvii] Shadburn, Cherokee Planters, 189-98.

[ccxxviii] NARA RG 393 m1475 r1 fr 0504.

[ccxxix] July 15, 1825, Hugh Montgomery to the Sec. of War, in Shadburn, Unhallowed Intrusion, 536.

[ccxxx] NA RG 92 Entry 350 Box 2, Vol. 2.

[ccxxxi] NA RG 92 Entry 350 Box 2 Vol. 2 260.

[ccxxxii] NA RG 92 Entry 352 Box 6.

[ccxxxiii] NA RG 92 Entry 352 Box 3.

[ccxxxiv] NA RG 92 Entry 350 Box 2.

[ccxxxv] NARA RG 393 m1475 r1 fr 0209-11.

[ccxxxvi] NARA RG 393 m1475 r1 fr 0651-53.

[ccxxxvii] NARA RG 393 m1475 r1 fr 0752-54.

[ccxxxviii] NARA RG 3993 m1475 r1 fr 0749-51.

[ccxxxix] NARA RG 393 m1475 r1 fr 0860-62.

[ccxl] NARA RG 393 m1475 r1 fr 0854-55. A Capt. N. P. Dodson belonged to Lindsay's regiment of Tennessee Mounted Volunteers.

[ccxli] NA RG 92 Entry 350 Box 2 Vol. 2 232.

[ccxlii] NA RG 92 Entry 352 Box 3.

[ccxliii] NA RG 92 Entry 350 Box 2 Vol. 2 280.

[ccxliv] NA RG 92 Entry 352 Box 3.

[ccxlv] NA RG 92 Entry 352 Box 3.

[ccxlvi] NARA RG 393 m1475 r1 fr 0209-11.

[ccxlvii] NARA RG 393 m1475 r1 fr 0536-37.

[ccxlviii] NA RG 92 Entry 350 Box 2 Vol. 2.

[ccxlix] NARA RG 393 m1475 r1 fr 0578-79; NA RG 92 Entry 352 Box 3.

[ccl] NA RG 92 Entry 352 Box 3.

[ccli] NARA RG 393 m12475 r2 fr 0578-79.

[cclii] NA RG 92 Entry 352 Box 3.

[ccliii] NARA RG 393 m1475 r1 fr 0572-77.

[ccliv] NA RG 92 Entry 350 Box 2 Vol. 2 337.

[cclv] NARA RG 393 m1475 r1 fr 0640-41; ibid, fr 0651-53.

[cclvi] NARA RG 393 m1475 r1 fr 0536-37.

[cclvii] July 25, 1836, Gen. Wool, Headquarters Army, to Capt. Vernon, Wool Letterbook, 52-3.

[cclviii] GDAH, Cherokee Letters, Talks, Treaties, Vol. 3, 597.

[cclix] July 23, 1836, Cornelius D. Terhune, Cassville, to Gov. William Schley, Document TCC584, http://neptune3.galib.uga.edu 07 April, 2003.

[cclx] For correspondence from Worcester during his imprisonment see Jack Frederick Kilpatrick and Anna Gritts Kilpatrick, eds., New Echota Letters (Dallas: Southern Methodist University Press, 1968), 95-103.

[cclxi] GDAH Letters and Orders of Gov. Gilmer, 1837-1838.

[cclxii] GDAH, Letters and orders of Gov. Gilmer, 1837-1838.

[cclxiii] GDAH Letters and Orders of Gov. Gilmer, 1837-1838.

[cclxiv] GDAH, Letters and Orders of Gov. Gilmer, 1837-1838.

[cclxv] NA RG 92 Entry 357 Box 6.

[cclxvi] NARA RG 393 m1475 r1 fr 0455.

[cclxvii] NA RG 92 Entry 350 Box 2, Vol. 2 261.

[cclxviii] NARA RG 393 m1475 r1 fr 0554-56.

[cclxix] NARA RG 393 m1475 r1 fr 0860-62.

[cclxx] NARA RG 393 m1475 r1 fr 0455.

[cclxxi] NA RG 92 Entry 352 Box 3.

[cclxxii] NA RG 92 Entry 352 Box 3.

[cclxxiii] NA RG 92 Entry 350 Box 2 Vol. 2.

[cclxxiv] NA RG 92 Entry 350 Box 2 Vol. 2 234.

[cclxxv] NA RG 92 Entry 350 Box 2 Vol. 2 261; NA RG 92 Entry 352 Box 3; NA RG 92 Entry 350 Box 2 Vol. 2 240.

[cclxxvi] NARA RG 393 m1475 r1 p. 137.

[cclxxvii] NARA RG 393 m14475 r1 fr 0637-39.

[cclxxviii] NARA RG 393 m1475 r1 fr 0455.

[cclxxix] NARA RG 393 m1475 r1 fr 0272-77.

[cclxxx] NARA RG 393 m1475 r1 fr 0492.

[cclxxxi] Don L. Shadburn, Unhallowed Intrusion, A History of Cherokee Families in Forsyth County, Georgia (Saline, MI: McNaughton and Gunn, 1993), 496-98.

[cclxxxii] Ibid, 498-501. Many standard histories of the Cherokees carry accounts of the missionaries' arrests.

[cclxxxiii] Ibid.

[cclxxxiv] George R. Gilmer, Sketches of Some of the First Settlers of Upper Georgia, of the Cherokees, and the Author (Americus, GA: Americus Book Company, 1926), 409.

[cclxxxv] Ibid, 492-96.

[cclxxxvi] Ibid, 503, 517-19.

[cclxxxvii] NARA RG 393 m1475 r1 fr 0286-89.

[cclxxxviii] NARA RG 393 m1475 r1 fr 0286.

[cclxxxix] NA RG 92 Entry 357 Box 6.

[ccxc] NARA RG 393 m1475 r1 fr 0286-89.

[ccxci] NARA RG 393 m1475 r1 fr 0286-89.

[ccxcii] GDAH Cherokee Letters, Talks, Treaties, Vol. 3, 750; NARA RG 393 m1475 r1 fr 0860-62.

ccxciii NARA RG 393 m1475 r1 fr 0286-89.

ccxciv NA RG 92 Entry 350 Box 2 Vol. 2 280.

ccxcv NARA RG 393 m1475 r1 fr 0286-89.

ccxcvi NARA RG 393 m1475 r1 fr 0286-87.

ccxcvii NARA RG 393 m1475 r1 p. 257.

ccxcviii GDAH Cherokee Letters, Talks, Treaties, Vol. 3, 210.

ccxcix See Shadburn, Unhallowed Intrusion, passim.

ccc Frances P. Stiles, "Large Stockade Built for Indians," Walker County Messenger, Nov. 5, 1915.

ccci Ibid.

cccii William G. McLoughlin, Cherokees and Missionaries, 1789-1839 (New Haven: Yale University Press, 1984), 314-15.

ccciii NA RG 92 Entry 350 Box 2 Vol. 2 215-16.

ccciv http://ftp.rootsweb.com, 8 October, 2004.

cccv Ibid.

cccvi NA RG 92 Entry 350 Box 2 Vol. 2 233.

cccvii GDAH, RG 1-1-5, Governor's Correspondence, Box 19. See also NA RG 92 Entry 357 Box 6.

cccviii NA RG 92 Entry 352 Box 3.

cccix NARA RG 393 m1475 r1 p. 237.

cccx Orders, Headquarters Georgia, May 7, 1838, Benjamin T. Watkins Collection, Mss. 717, Box 1, Folder 3, Special Collections, Woodruff Libraries, Emory University, Atlanta.

cccxi 16 May, 1838, Requisition of Capt. Benj. T. Watkins, Benjamin T. Watkins Collection, Mss. 717, Box 1, Folder 3, Special Collections, Robert W. Woodruff Library, Emory University, Atlanta.

cccxii NARA RG 393 m1475 r1 p. 574

cccxiii 9 June, 1838, Benj. T. Watkins, Commanding, Ft. Cumming, to Commanding Officer, Middle Military District, Benjamin T. Watkins Collection, Mss. 717, Box 1, Folder 3, Special Collections, Robert W. Woodruff Library, Emory University, Atlanta.

cccxiv 17 June, 1838, Floyd, N. Echota to Capt. Watkins, Benjamin T. Watkins Collection, Mss. 717, Box 1, Folder 3, Special Collections, Robert W. Woodruff Library, Emory University, Atlanta .

cccxv 18 June, 1838, Brig. Gen. Floyd, New Echota, Orders No. 31, Benjamin T. Watkins Collection, Mss. 717, Box 1, Folder 3, Special Collections, Robert W. Woodruff Library, Emory University, Atlanta.

cccxvi NARARG 393 m1475 r1 fr 0665-66

cccxvii GDAH Letters and Orders of Gov. Gilmer 1837-1838

cccxviii NARA RG 393 m1475 r1 fr 0915-17

cccxix NARA RG 393 m1475 r1 p. 257.

cccxx Butrick Journal p. 3

cccxxi Cherokee Claims Skin Bayou District p. 59

cccxxii "Detailed Account of the Skirmishes Around LaFayette," Walker County Messenger Friday Nov. 5, 1915, p. 4

cccxxiii NA RG 92 Entry 350 Box 2 Vol 2 Letterbook p 236

cccxxiv NA RG 92 Entry 352 Box 3

cccxxv NARA RG 393 m1475 r1 p.137a, b

cccxxvi NA RG 92 Entry 352 Box 3 Letters received 1838-1845

cccxxvii 10 May, 1838, Benjamin T. Watkins Collection, Mss. 717, Box 1, Folder 3, Special Collections, Robert W. Woodruff Library, Emory University, Atlanta.

cccxxviii 16 May, 1838, Requisition of Capt. Benj. T. Watkins, Benjamin T. Watkins Collection, Mss. 717, Box 1, Folder 3, Special Collections, Robert W. Woodruff Library, Emory University, Atlanta.

cccxxix 24 June, 1838, A. Cox, Benjamin T. Watkins Collection, Mss. 717, Box 1, Folder 3, Special Collections, Robert W. Woodruff Library, Emory University, Atlanta.

cccxxx 25 May, 1838, Benjamin T. Watkins Collection, Mss. 717, Box 1, Folder 3, Special Collections, Robert W. Woodruff Library, Emory University, Atlanta.

cccxxxi 24 June, 1838, Benjamin T. Watkins Collection, Mss. 717, Box 1, Folder 3, Special Collections, Robert W. Woodruff Library, Emory University, Atlanta.

cccxxxii NARA RG 393 m1475 r1 fr 0637-39

cccxxxiii NA RG 92 Entry 350 Box 2 Vol 2 Letterbook p 309

cccxxxiv Butrick Journal p. 3

cccxxxv NARA RG 393 m1475 r1 p. 574

cccxxxvi Wm. P. Giles, Ft. Poinsett, to the Officer Commanding at Fort Cummings [sic], Benjamin T. Watkins Collection, Mss. 717, Box 1, Folder 3, Special Collections, Robert W. Woodruff Library, Emory University, Atlanta.

cccxxxvii 9 June, 1838, Benj. Watkins, Ft. Cumming, to Commanding Officer, Middle Military District, Benjamin T. Watkins Collection, Mss. 717, Box 1, Folder 3, Special Collections, Robert W. Woodruff Library, Emory University, Atlanta.

cccxxxviii 9 June, 1838, Benj. T. Watkins, Capt., Ft. Cumming, to Lt. Wood, Benjamin T. Watkins Collection, Mss. 717, Box 1, Folder 3, Special Collections, Robert W. Woodruff Library, Emory University, Atlanta.

cccxxxix GDAH, Correspondence of Gov. Gilmer, 197.

cccxl NA RG 92 Entry 357 Box 6.

cccxli GDAH Ga. Military Vol. 9 p94

cccxlii NARA RG 393 m1475 r1 fr 0209-11; NARA RG 393 m1475 r1 fr 0256-57.

cccxliii NARA RG 393 m1475 r1 fr 0475

cccxliv NARA RG 393 m1475 r1 fr 0860-62

cccxlv GDAH Ga. Military Vol. 9 p94

cccxlvi NARA RG 393 m1475 r1 fr 0319-22

cccxlvii NA RG 350 Box 2 Vol. 2

cccxlviii NARA RG 393 m1475 r1 p 137

cccxlix NARA RG 393 m1475 r1 fr 0637-39

cccl NARA RG 393 m1475 r1 fr 0319-22

cccli NARA RG 393 m1475 r1 fr 0405

ccclii NARA RG 393 m1475 r1 fr 0455

cccliii NARA RG 393 m1475 r1 fr 0572-75

cccliv NARA RG 393 m1475 r1 fr 0554-56

ccclv Polk County History as Written and Prepared by Dr. Charles K. Henderson, 1897, chapter 3 p. 1, trans. by Mary Read, www.rootsweb.com, 19 November, 2003.

ccclvi Ibid, p. 2.

ccclvii Shadburn, Cherokee Planters, 275.

ccclviii See, for examples, 1842 Cherokee Claims Saline District, comp. by Marybelle Chase, 12, 15, 16, 18, 20, 22-4, 27, 28, 31, 55, 68, 72.

ccclix Ibid, 22.

ccclx Henderson, Polk County History, 2.

ccclxi GDAH, Cherokee Letters Talks Treaties, Vol. 3, 654.

ccclxii GDAH RG 1-1-5 Box 19.

ccclxiii NARA RG 393 m1475 r1 fr 0283.

ccclxiv GDAH Cherokee Letters Talks Treaties vol. 3 722.

ccclxv NARA RG 393 m1475 r1 fr 0372-73.

ccclxvi NARA RG 393 m1475 r1 fr 0572-74.

ccclxvii GDAH, RG 1-1-5, Box 19.

ccclxviii NA RG 92 Entry 357 Box 6.

ccclxix NARA RG 393 m1475 r1 fr 0260-62.

ccclxx NARA RG 393 m1475 r1 fr 0209-11.

ccclxxi Isaac S. Vincent Papers, Mss. 617, Folder 6, Hargrett Library, University of Georgia Libraries, Athens.

ccclxxii May, 1838, Miller Grieve, Milledgeville, to Capt. Isaac S. Vincent, http://neptune3.galib.uga.edu, 15 March, 2001.

ccclxxiii NARA RG 393 m1475 r1 fr 0363.

ccclxxiv Feb. 5, 1839, Augustus H. Stokes, Newton, to Isaac Vincent, http://neptune3.galib.uga.edu, 7 July, 2002.

ccclxxv NA RG 92 Entry 350 Box 2 Vol 2 215-216.

ccclxxvi NARA RG 393 m1475 r1 137.

ccclxxvii NARA RG 393 m21475 r1 fr 0351-53.

ccclxxviii May 20, 1838 Headquarters Eastern Division, Order 30 http://neptune3.galib.uga.edu, 7 July, 2002.

ccclxxix May 28-June 26, 1838, Cedar Town Provision Returns, http://neptune3.galib.uga.edu, 7 July, 2002.

ccclxxx NARA RG 393 m1475 r1 fr 0637-39.

ccclxxxi June 14, 1838, Gen. Floyd, Cedar Town, to Capt. Isaac Vincent, http://neptune3.galib.uga.edu, 7 July, 2002.

ccclxxxii June 14, 1838 Gen. Floyd, Cedar Town, to Capt. Vincent, http://neptune3.galib.uga.edu, 7 July, 2002.

ccclxxxiii June 21, 1838, Gen. Floyd, New Echota, to Capt. Vincent, http://neptune3.galib.uga.edu, 7 July, 2002.

ccclxxxiv May 28-June 26, 1838, Cedar Town Provision Returns, http://neptune3.galib.uga.edu, 7 July, 2002.

ccclxxxv Shadburn, Cherokee Planters, 124.

ccclxxxvi July 25, 1836, John E. Wool , headquarters Army, to Maj. M. M. Payne, Wool Letterbook, 59.

ccclxxxvii Sept. 28, 1836, John E. Wool, Headquarters Army, to Maj. M. M. Payne, Wool Letterbook, 142-43.

ccclxxxviii 1842 Cherokee Claims, Tahlequah District, 36, 37, 171, 194, 195.

ccclxxxix Aug. 27, 1836, John E. Wool, Headquarters Army, to Maj. C. H. Nelson, Wool Letterbook, 81-2.

cccxc Sept. 28, 1836, John E. Wool, Head Quarters Army, to Maj. M. M. Payne, Wool Letterbook, 154.

cccxci Sept. 28, 1836, John E. Wool, Head Quarters Army, to Maj. M. M. Payne, Wool Letterbook, 142-43.

cccxcii Sept. 28, 1836, John E. Wool, Headquarters Army, to Maj. M. M. Payne, Wool Letterbook, 142-43.

cccxciii Feb. 26, 1841, Samuel Stewart, Rome, to Gov. Charles McDonald, http://neptune3.galib.uga.edu, 7 July, 2002.

cccxciv NARA RG 393 m1475 r1 fr 0268-69.

cccxcv NARA RG 393 m1475 r1 fr 0363.

cccxcvi NARA RG 393 m1475 r1 fr0272-77.

cccxcvii June 19, 1836, William J. W. Wellborn, Milledgeville, to Gov. William Schley, http://neptune3.galib.uga.edu, 7 July, 2003.

cccxcviii Sept. 28, 1836, John E. Wool, Headquarters Army, to Maj. M. M. Payne, Wool Letterbook, 143.

cccxcix GDAH, Letters and orders of Gov. Gilmer, 1837-1838.

cd Sept. 28, 1836, John E. Wool, Headquarters Army, to Gen. Jesup, Wool Letterbook, 144-45.

cdi NARA RG 393 m1475 r1 fr 0386-87.

cdii GDAH Letters and Orders of Gov. Gilmer 1837-1838.

cdiii NA RG 92 Entry 350 Box 2 Vol. 2, 234.

cdiv NARA RG 393 m1475 r1 fr 0351-53.

cdv NARA RG 393 m1475 r1 fr 0637-39.

cdvi Sept. 28, 1836, John E. Wool, Headquarters Army, to Maj. M. M. Payne, Wool Letterbook, 143.

cdvii NARA RG 393 m1475 r1 fr 0405; NARA RG 393, m1475 r1 fr 0272-79.

cdviii NARA RG 393 m1475 r1 fr 0239-42.

cdix NA G 92 Entry 350 Box 2 Vol. 2 311.

cdx NA RG 92 Entry 357 Box 6.

cdxi NA RG 92 Entry 352 Box 3.

cdxii NA RG 92 Entry 350 Box 2 Vol. 2 331.

cdxiii NA RG 92 Entry 350 Box 2 Vol. 2 311.

cdxiv NA RG 92 Entry 350 Box 2 Vol. 2.

cdxv NA RG 92 Entry 352 Box 3.

cdxvi NA RG 92 Entry 350 Box 2 Vol. 2 325.

cdxvii NA RG 92 Entry 352 Box 3.

cdxviii NA RG 92 Entry 350 Box 2 Vol. 2 331.

cdxix NARA RG 393 m1475 r1 fr 0478-79.

Made in the USA
Lexington, KY
22 July 2013